SPOTLIGHT ON
SPECIAL EDUCATIONAL NEEDS:

EMOTIONAL AND BEHAVIOURAL DIFFICULTIES

JONATHAN FOGELL AND ROB LONG

A NASEN Publication

Published in 1997

ISBN 0 906730 93 7

Published by NASEN Enterprises Ltd.
NASEN Enterprises is a company limited by guarantee, registered in England and Wales.
Company No. 2637438.

Further copies of this book and details of NASEN's many other publications may be obtained from the Publications Department at its registered office:
NASEN House, 4/5, Amber Business Village, Amber Close, Amington, Tamworth, Staffs. B77 4RP.
Tel: 01827 311500; Fax: 01827 313005; email: welcome@nasen.org.uk

Copy editing by Nicola von Schreiber.
Cover design by Graphic Images.
Typeset in Times by J. C. Typesetting and printed in the United Kingdom by J. H. Brookes, Stoke-on-Trent.

SPOTLIGHT ON SPECIAL EDUCATIONAL NEEDS: EMOTIONAL AND BEHAVIOURAL DIFFICULTIES

Contents

Acknowledgments

The authors wish to thank their respective families for their support and patience during the compilation of this book. In addition the support and constructive criticism received from a number of people, especially from Dorothy Smith and the other members of the NASEN Publications Committee, was extremely helpful. They would also like to thank all those colleagues in their respective LEAs, Devon and West Sussex, who have given encouragement and advice during the compilation of this book.

SPOTLIGHT ON SPECIAL EDUCATIONAL NEEDS: EMOTIONAL AND BEHAVIOURAL DIFFICULTIES

Introduction

This handbook aims to offer practical advice to special educational needs co-ordinators (SENCOs) and class teachers. It will also be of interest to SEN classroom support assistants, SEN governors, and parents of children with emotional and behavioural difficulties. It is one in a series of NASEN books aimed at providing support for teachers in implementing the recommendations of the *Code of Practice on the Identification and Assessment of Special Educational Needs* (1994). It is intended for both primary and secondary schools.

This book aims
to enable the reader to have greater
INSIGHT & UNDERSTANDING
into the causes and nature of
emotional and behavioural difficulties
and to become increasingly
COMPETENT & EFFECTIVE
in responding to them appropriately
to help all of their pupils to be
CONFIDENT & ACHIEVING

Emotional and Behavioural Difficulties as a Special Educational Need

The main aim of schools is to help pupils learn. The National Curriculum now provides a framework with both content and targets to which a wide range of learning approaches can be related. Many pupils face barriers which prevent or hinder their learning. Cognitive/sensory and physical difficulties which affect learning are readily appreciated. We are now becoming more aware of the barriers faced by children with emotional and behavioural difficulties.

There has been a long tradition of responding to such children as being 'naughty' and in need of increased control or punishment. While it is true that establishing clear boundaries and a framework of rewards and sanctions is important, the sad fact is that the problems experienced by some children go far beyond naughtiness. A significant minority of pupils confound the most experienced of their teachers by an apparent inability to respond positively and consistently to adult controls.

A Framework Based on Principles

This book provides a description of emotional and behavioural difficulties (EBD) as they are manifested in classrooms and other learning situations and gives details on how they are encompassed in legislation. It provides a framework for understanding emotional and behavioural difficulties based on the following three principles:

1. that all human behaviour results from an individual's response to complicated webs of influence.

   Environment: family, school ethos, teachers, neighbourhood community, and culture influences like the media and their peers.

   Child: the child's underlying temperament, personality and stage of intellectual/emotional development.

   Emotional and behavioural difficulties can therefore be as much about the situation or context as they are about the child;

2. that parents, schools and communities make a difference in every young person's life. No child should be seen as a lost cause. No matter how problematic a child's past experiences and no matter how difficult the behaviour they present, there will always be opportunities to effect improvements by systematic, sympathetic handling of the problem. Even where a school does not have the resources to meet a child's needs, the adoption of consistent approaches will inform any subsequent school placement about the child's strengths and weaknesses and they will be able to plan effectively to meet the child's needs;

3. that emotional and behavioural difficulties can present challenging dilemmas for the school. Where a child presents behaviour which impinges on the rights of other children to safety and the opportunity to learn effectively, or where a child consistently damages the learning environment, difficult choices sometimes have to be made. In circumstances where a child presents ongoing patterns of behaviour which interfere with the well-being of themselves, other children or staff members, then responsibility for that child must be shared by the whole school.

There are several reasons why understanding and supporting these pupils is made more difficult than those with such challenges as physical or sensory impairments.

1. The behaviour (it always has to be behaviour as we cannot directly observe emotions) that concerns us may not always happen as and when expected.

2. Problem behaviours may also depend on the presence or absence of certain adults and how they respond.

3. Many of the behaviours that concern us are 'typically' normal features for all children from time to time.

4. It is extremely difficult to identify the precise causes of EBD because we know that there can be more than one plausible explanation. Family issues, personality, teaching style, peer relationships, medical reasons, can each offer some rationale for a child's problem behaviour.

5. The impact problem behaviour has on the well-being of the adults working with them. An over-active or badly behaved child drains the energy of adults but also badly affects their feelings of personal competence and effectiveness. Children with EBD are thus less likely to engender positive sympathy and empathy from adults than children with other types of SEN. Of course children with EDB are not the only ones with this experience. Those working with children with hearing impairments and moderate learning difficulties will have experienced times when the child's special needs have not been acknowledged and their behaviour interpreted negatively.

Core Assumptions
- Behaviour is always a management issue.

- Children are trying to solve problems not be problems.

- The way to change a child's behaviour is to change how we respond to them.

- Learning is best when pupils are positively rewarded and respected.

- Supporting pupils may involve developing new skills.

- An agreed plan of action followed by all adults in the school is essential.

- Pupils need to know what behaviour is expected in different circumstances.

- The consequences for appropriate and inappropriate behaviour should be known to all involved.

- The emotional and behavioural difficulties may be singly caused or multi-factorial.

When we are faced with a child presenting behavioural difficulties we have to respond in some way. In supporting children who face such difficulties it is not always necessary to know the cause, but a working hypothesis will help inform us and enable the most useful strategies to be selected. How teachers and other support staff help such children overcome/cope with these learning barriers is the central theme of this book.

The problems faced by any particular child will be largely unique to that child. Treating children with problems as types with prescribed methods of 'treatment' is a well-documented problem for teachers. Labels bring stigma which presents its own set of educational difficulties.

Troubled and/or Troublesome Pupils?

The term 'emotional and behavioural difficulties' has almost become synonymous for those pupils who are 'acting out', behaving in challenging/disruptive ways. These children are often described as having conduct disorders. They have tended to take a greater share of the school's focus and energies. As a matter of expediency teachers tend to be more concerned with behavioural than with emotional difficulties. There are also those children who 'act in', presenting isolated, depressed, anxious and withdrawn behaviour. These children are often described as having emotional disorders.

Both groups of children have special educational needs in as much as they are experiencing barriers to their learning, and are likely to benefit from structured programmes of support, which can be detailed and monitored through the *Code of Practice*. In drawing a distinction between broadly acting out and acting in children, it always needs to be remembered that pupils who are acting out may also be experiencing poor self-esteem, and depression. This book will give equal weight to the needs of both broad groupings and give suggestions about how schools can offer support.

The authors will therefore refer to broad descriptors of behavioural patterns from which teachers can draw strategies to build up individual programmes with which to respond to the problem behaviour and not the problem child. The class teacher's or form tutor's experience and training and knowledge of the pupil group will help to select appropriate strategies and to adapt them to individual needs. In designing support for a child with EBD it is expected that practitioners will seek a 'best fit' for their own circumstances.

Chapter 1 of this book gives a brief overview of the current framework of SEN legislation and related DfEE guidance. The rest of the book suggests strategies for working with pupils primarily at Stages 1 to 3 of the *Code of Practice* recommendations. The underlying principles of the strategies used do not, however, differ markedly from one stage to another. As a child progresses along the continuum it is more likely that there will be changes to:

- the pupil : teacher or classroom : support assistant ratio;

- the size of teaching groups;

- the amount of possible 1:1 work with the pupil;

- the clarity of objectives aimed at the concerns;

- amount and detail of record keeping;

- the background information on a child;

- the range of different professionals/therapists who have worked with or are currently working with the child.

Characteristics

The children we are going to be concerned with in this book are often the least liked and least understood of all children with special educational needs. For those children who are:

Acting out: their behaviour can be aggressive, threatening and disruptive: demanding of attention and preventing us from teaching other children.

Acting in: their emotional difficulties result in unresponsive or even self-damaging behaviour; they will appear to be anxious, depressed, withdrawn, passive and unmotivated. Their apparent irrational refusal to respond and co-operate may cause enormous frustration for teacher and fellow pupils.

Children with emotional and behavioural difficulties usually:

- are unhappy, unwilling and/or unable;

- receive less praise through their work and have fewer positive child/adult interactions;

- have learning difficulties or are under-achieving;

- have poor social skills and few friends;

- have a poor self-regard;

- are emotionally volatile;

- are easily hurt.

Not all of these features will be apparent on first encountering the child. Children need to protect their psychological well-being and so will go to great lengths to create an image that they are coping, or that their problems are someone else's fault or someone else's responsibility. More than anything this book stresses that despite the considerable efforts they make to conceal their problems, often rejecting help and support, those children with emotional and behavioural difficulties are the most vulnerable in our schools.

Chapter 1 – The Development of a Legal Framework

> Children with emotional and behavioural difficulties have special educational needs. In the terms of the legislation they have 'learning difficulties' because they are facing barriers which cause them to have significantly greater difficulties in learning than most of their peers.
>
> (DfEE *Circular 9/94* Section 4)

Emotional and behavioural difficulties were identified as a source of 'learning difficulty' by the *Warnock Report* (1978). Before that time children presenting difficult to manage behaviour were deemed maladjusted, under one of the ten categories of handicap identified under the *Education Act 1944*. Special school provision for maladjusted pupils grew at an enormous rate throughout the 1950s and 60s. In 1950, 587 pupils were attending special schools for maladjusted children. By 1970 the number had increased to 8,952 (Laslett, 1977). The *Underwood Report* (1955) provided much of the impetus for the development of provision for pupils with emotional and behavioural difficulties.

The 1994 *Code of Practice on the Identification and Assessment of Special Educational Needs,* marked a distinctive point in the development of approaches to emotional and behavioural difficulties. It included it as one of the eight broad groupings under which indicative questions can be addressed in the statutory assessment process. The *Code of Practice* does however stress that a child's learning difficulty may encompass more than one area of need and always will relate to the particular circumstances of the individual child. To that extent each special educational need is unique.

More detailed advice on approaches to working with pupils who have EBD is contained in *Circular 9/94: The Education of Children with Emotional and Behavioural Difficulties* (DfEE and the Department of Health). It includes detailed advice on the early identification of EBD in mainstream schools; recording by schools; seeking specialist advice; EBD in special schools; and issues e.g. psychiatric care, the particular needs of the very young, girls and young women.

Throughout the years there have been many attempts to define maladjustment as a discrete area of handicap (see the discussion of this under section Elusive Definitions). Attempts to achieve a consensus have been largely fruitless although there are still some checklists available that give criteria for assessment and a maladjustment or EBD rating at the end of the process. While such measures (e.g. *The Rutter Scale, The Bristol Social Adjustment Guide* or *The Devereaux Scales*) give some idea of the difference between a child's general behaviour and that, largely, of their peers, they provide little insight into the complex individual difficulties affecting the child which were referred to in the introduction.

A significant difficulty faced by the teacher when describing a child's behaviour as problematic is the ordinariness of some of the behaviour under concern. All children argue, call names, get upset, lose concentration etc. Teachers are acutely aware of the dangers of labeling and the possibility of a 'self-fulfilling prophecy' effect. To a certain extent this can be overcome by a constant attempt to focus on the behaviour and not the child as the problem. In the end the teacher is faced with a judgment to make about when to address an inappropriate behaviour, and perhaps when planned ignoring is more appropriate. The teacher's difficulty is illustrated by the comment of a Brighton head teacher who stated:

Children with emotional and behavioural difficulties are just like any other children only more so.

In this book we shall promote the notion of emotional and behavioural difficulties as a judgment on the behaviour which a child presents and the circumstances under which that behaviour is seen as a problem. Such an approach was summed up by Michael Roe (1978):

Some have never been taught how to behave appropriately. Some have experienced life circumstances that nobody should be expected to put up with. In almost every case there is a child who has dug themself into a hole they can't get out of.

He went on to say, 'When we describe behaviour as maladjusted we are making a judgment about situations.'

The teacher's and school's response to emotional and behavioural difficulties now comes under the aegis of the *Education Act 1996*. Like all areas of education there has been a period of considerable change throughout the 1980s and 90s.

Statutory Changes 1980–1993

The major changes in legislation relating to pupils with special educational needs since 1980 are detailed in *Figure 1*. It is probable that education will be subject to even more change over the next few years. The publication of the *Dearing Report* on the National Curriculum was aimed at presenting a five-year moratorium on significant changes in education but the ongoing issues raised by the educational inspectorate, OFSTED; issues emerging from the settling-in process of the *Code of Practice* and changes on the political scene all make the stabilising of educational policy development look somewhat remote. Of course, if development slowed down too much there would be cries of stagnation as a problem in the educational service.

The changes to the regulations on special educational needs through the *Education Act 1993* came about largely as a response to the joint HMI/Audit Commission Report in 1989. This described the following flaws with the *1981 Education Act* and associated SEN procedures:

- lack of clarity in definition of special educational needs and lack of adequate policies in mainstream schools;

- wide variations in the way different LEAs interpreted the Act;

- lack of accountability between parents and schools, schools and LEAs, parents and LEAs;

- great discrepancies between LEAs in time taken to complete statements;

- lack of central government incentives to LEAs to improve SEN performance;

- the appeals process was too slow and cumbersome;

- children with SEN but without statements were getting inadequate provision.

1980 Act Composition of Governing Bodies	Establishing individual governing bodies for most schools.
1981 Act Special Educational Needs	Introduced the notion of SEN, abolished categories, emphasis on learning difficulties and individual needs, introduced statements.
1986 Act New composition and powers of governing bodies	Laid down the size, constitution and function of governing bodies in detail in relation to curriculum.
1988 Education Reform Act	Brought about the following changes: The National Curriculum; re-emphasis on Christian background to religious education; open enrollment; grant maintained status; city technology colleges; LMSS.

1992 Schools Act	OFSTED. The Office for Standards in Education created to work with Her Majesty's inspectors. Regular inspections. Schools need to respond to inspectors' reports to parents.
Education Act 1993	Its main elements make it easier for schools to become GM; creation of the Funding Agency for Schools (FAS); encouragement of specialisation for schools; set-up of SCAA; change in regulations relating to: Religious education Sex education Special educational needs Exclusions Removal of surplus places Identification of failing schools
1994 The Code of Practice	Concerning the identification and assessment of special educational needs.
1994 The SEN Tribunal	Introduced a systematic process by which parents could appeal against LEA decisions through an independent process.
Education Act 1996	Unified the provisions of the *1944 Act* and the *1993 Act*. Largely left the provisions of the *1993 Act* unchanged but incorporated the provisions of the *1996 Disability Discrimination Act* requiring schools to develop access action plans. Also the application of the *Code of Practice* to nursery education.

Figure 1

The *Children Act* in England and Wales was introduced in 1989. Legislation in Scotland followed in 1995. This embodied many of the principles of the *1981 Act*:

• the welfare of the child to be paramount in all decision making;

• continuing parental responsibility;

• partnership between parents and local authorities;

• the importance of families for children;

• the importance of listening to the views of the children and parents.

1989 was also the year of the *Elton Report* into discipline in schools. Amongst its conclusions was the assertion that schools were generally orderly but much was needed in training of staff and the development of policies towards discipline. It stressed the strong link between curriculum content and delivery and discipline. The *Elton Report* made 172 separate recommendations covering the expectations and responsibilities of head teacher, teachers, the Secretary of State, parents, pupils, the police, schools governors, local education authorities and the government. There were a number of initiatives throughout the country to respond to the *Elton Report*. Its biggest impact has been in shaping the advice given to schools through DfEE Circulars, especially 10/94 dealing with *Pupil Behaviour and Discipline* and 10/94 dealing with *Exclusions from School*.

There appear to be two potentially conflicting trends behind much of the recent legislation. The laws aimed towards schools and teacher effectiveness from the *1988 Act* onwards have introduced greater autonomy, accountability and performance targets aimed at developing the organisational culture of the school. SEN legislation reflected by the *Code of Practice* and Circulars such as *Pupils with Problems* have required schools to take a more individually focused approach to children's needs. There is much evidence to indicate that some of the whole school measures, e.g. open enrolments, league tables based on exam results, have tended to make life more difficult for children with SEN. Certainly children with EBD have been affected by this process with consistent rises in the rate of pupil exclusions from schools through the 1990s and an acknowledgment that many children with statements of SEN are amongst those excluded (Hayden ESRC 1996).

The *Code of Practice*

The *Code of Practice* was published in 1994. It described the roles, responsibilities and procedures relating to the *Education Act 1993* (which now apply unchanged to the *Education Act 1996*). The *Code* recognises a continuum of special educational needs and describes five clear stages of response by the schools and LEA. The first three stages are largely the responsibility of the school with some support provided from external sources. The final two stages are the responsibility of the LEA. The *Code of Practice* spells out the roles and responsibilities of teachers, schools, LEAs and associated bodies. *Figure 2* gives a breakdown of the requirements of the different stages of the *Code of Practice* continuum. For a detailed description of the implications of the *Code of Practice* refer to the NASEN publication *Procedures and Practice for Special Educational Needs Co-ordinators* (Smith, 1996).

The Code of Practice Stages
Stage 1 - The child's needs are identified and assessed by the class teacher. In secondary schools, subject teachers and form tutors share this responsibility. Concerns are recorded on the school's SEN register by the SENCO (Special educational needs co-ordinator).
Stage 2 - Parents are consulted. An individual education plan (IEP) is drawn up and monitored by the SENCO. (Some external assessment may be sought at this stage e.g. behavioural support advisory service, speech and language therapist etc.)
Stage 3 - Parents are consulted. A more detailed IEP is drawn up describing a school-based intervention which will involve more detailed assessment and/or intervention by external support agency (behaviour support team, educational psychologist, child guidance clinic, social services department).
Stage 4 - The local education authority carries out a statutory assessment of special educational needs seeking detailed involvement and reports from parents, schools, area medical officer, social services department and any other body which the LEA considers desirable.
Stage 5 - The LEA draws up a statement of special educational needs which describes the child's educational needs and the provision which will be made to meet those needs. The statement of SEN must be reviewed annually.

Figure 2

The *Code of Practice* provides a framework for assessing and monitoring pupils' behaviour which is of concern to teachers or parents, and which is a barrier to learning. It suggests a range of evidence needed by an LEA before they consider undertaking further assessment of a child's special educational needs. The range of evidence sought by LEAs, before instigating statutory assessment in response to emotional and behavioural difficulties, is discussed in Chapter 6. The suggestions made throughout this book, will support teachers in making an effective intervention through the *Code of Practice*.

Chapter 2 – Emotional and Behavioural Difficulties in the School Context

As we have indicated, emotional and behavioural difficulties arise from a variety of causes and there are many plausible explanations for a child's difficulties. It is not surprising that when teachers misinterpret the signals given by a child the response strategies they adopt are usually less effective. A trial and error approach is often necessary and it may lessen frustration as setbacks are encountered if this is understood from the outset. It is most important to acknowledge the difficulties if you are going to address them. It is less important to apportion blame. (In the 'blame game' there are seldom any winners.) It is helpful, however, to explore aspects of the children's daily lives which may contribute to their difficulties and seek to change those features or antecedents.

Making Sense of Emotional and Behavioural Difficulties

No single cause exists to explain childhood emotional and behavioural difficulties, but there are some that seem to be more readily understandable, for example:

- a child who is grieving the loss of a parent may become aggressive and challenging;

- a child experiencing some form of distress may withdraw or display other emotional difficulties.

At other times the causes are perplexing and not readily identifiable. Most often (in the jargon), the causes can be multi-factorial.

Discussions around emotional and behavioural difficulties can often be emotive. Issues around child rearing approaches are always controversial. There is no other form of special educational needs which leads intelligent people to say 'the child needs a clip around the ear hole' (or worse) but such remedies can often be heard in relation to behaviour difficulties. That is not surprising because, as we readily acknowledge, the behaviours which cause concern are often hurtful, threatening or damaging. Our belief in the value of having some understanding of these behaviours does not mean that we are condoning them.

A key point which cannot be over-emphasised is that schools do make a difference.

> The rate of disruption and delinquency differs between schools more than the characteristics of their pupil intake would predict.

Most children with emotional and behavioural difficulties respond well to suitable in-school programmes. Children mature and the impact of certain stressors dissipates over time. Many overcome their difficulties with no formal behaviour strategies used (spontaneous remission). Some even overcome their difficulties despite the use of behavioural programmes.

Elusive Definitions

There is not and can never be a fixed definition of 'emotional and behavioural difficulties'. It is a relative concept in that its meaning varies between observers and across time and place. Our individual understanding of any specific behaviour will depend upon its frequency, duration, intensity, abnormality and effect on us and others. How 'I' feel as the observer will also affect my response. The behaviour we are concerned with is on a continuum from behaviour which may challenge us but is within the normal range, to behaviour which is commonly associated with some form of mental disturbance. We are concerned with behaviour which becomes unacceptable through a child being distressed, having failed to learn the appropriate rules and expectations, or seemingly to have willfully chosen to refuse to comply with reasonable adult requests.

Checklists of Indicative Behaviours

As indicated earlier, checklists of indicative behaviours are fraught with dangers because they suggest that certain behaviours are implicitly problematic. That is clearly not so simple in the school. Judgments need to be made about the context of the behaviour as well as the actual behaviour. The child who runs down a corridor screaming at the top of their voice could be presenting inappropriate behaviour. If they are running down the corridor screaming at the top of their voice that somebody has had a serious accident on the playground and the teacher on duty needs help from their colleagues then that behaviour suddenly becomes seen as highly appropriate. The following list of behaviours which might cause concern needs to be viewed through the filter of the above statement. The child with emotional and behavioural difficulties might present the following problem behaviours in two or more educational environments:

The pupil:

1. reacts negatively to changes in routine or teaching staff;
2. shows physically or verbally aggressive behaviour to staff or other pupils;
3. shows aggressive behaviour to classroom pressures;
4. becomes excessively withdrawn in reaction to the above circumstances;
5. reacts inappropriately to correction or praise;
6. has a poor ability to sustain appropriate relationships with his age peers;
7. persistently breaks the school rules;
8. presents excessively sensitive behaviour (crying and whining in response to trivial events);
9. exhibits low levels of on-task behaviour;
10. exhibits excessive mood swings;
11. goes to extreme lengths to attract attention;
12. provokes or distracts other pupils from their work;
13. is a persistent truant or frequently absconds from school;
14. presents behaviour likely to be injurious to them, other pupils, staff, equipment or the fabric of the building.

Key Factors Which May Cause Problem Behaviour
(You will note that at all times we are writing about problem behaviours rather than problem pupils.)

Classroom Organisation   Within pupil

PROBLEM BEHAVIOUR

Family   Influences on teacher

Children are very complicated little people and we should not be surprised that they experience difficulties from time to time. Neither should we be surprised that these difficulties can be caused for many reasons. A bit like back-aches. We may each experience back-aches, but for many different reasons. Because we can never deal completely with the entire child, our focus is always on the behaviour. In school the focus will be on those behaviours which are preventing pupils from learning. If we take the view that our school is OK and that the problem is the pupil's then we will develop a school which REACTS.

This contrasts with those characteristics found when we accept that behaviour is always a management issue, and that there will always be some behaviours we wish to increase, and some we wish to decrease. This will now lead to a school which is PROACTIVE. Such schools attempt to anticipate potential difficulties and adjust their programmes and procedures in the light of forward planning. Of course, it is impossible to anticipate all eventualities but it is possible to anticipate a number of obvious difficulties if you plan ahead. Schools can be rated on each dimension. (See *Figure 3*.) Teachers may ask: 'Are we where we want to be on each continuum?'

You can see that taking a problem behaviour view is much more empowering to all concerned. It means that we all share responsibility to improve difficult situations, not just one side. It promotes a win-win situation. We reflect this view when we say, 'condemn the act, not the child.'

Family-Based Difficulties
The child's family will exert enormous influence on a child's emotional and behavioural development.

1. As families pass through various developmental changes, such as children going to school, they can get stuck. A child may develop emotional and/or behavioural difficulties as a means of 'helping' the family through this.

2. A child's position in the family can affect their personality and behaviour. First-born children can come to expect to be in charge and feel frustration and anger if they are not. Middle-born children can feel resentful towards other siblings. Later-born children can come to feel inadequate as they are surrounded by others who are better able in all things. These are not 'unchangeable facts' but examples of what can happen.

3. A family's parenting skills may be poor and result in children failing to learn the consequences for their behaviour. They can come to behave impulsively and without any apparent appreciation of what will happen to them.

Problem Pupil		Problem Behaviour
REACTIVE Deals with crisis situations Finds culprit when trouble occurs	< 1 2 3 4 5 >	PROACTIVE Plans strategies to pre-empt problem behaviour
CONFRONTATIONAL Depends on sanctions to control undesired behaviour; emphasis on labeling, reprimand and punishment	< 1 2 3 4 5 >	POSITIVE Catches spontaneous positive behaviour and rewards it; emphasis on identifying good models of behaviour
FAULT FINDING Believes that the pupils or their parents must change first	< 1 2 3 4 5 >	INITIATING Involves all staff, pupils, parents to achieve shared aims
INDIVIDUALIST Each teacher depends on their own resources	< 1 2 3 4 5 >	COLLABORATIVE Whole school policies developed
AUTHORITARIAN Minimal involvement of pupils, parents or staff team in decision making	< 1 2 3 4 5 >	DEMOCRATIC All staff, pupils and parents actively involved
STATUS FOCUSED Concern is with behaviour that challenges staff authority	< 1 2 3 4 5 >	WELFARE FOCUSED Concern is on relationships between staff and pupils

Figure 3 (Adapted from Dorling 1993)

Classroom Management/Organisational Difficulties

Behaviour is always a management issue. The professional requirements upon all teachers mean they cannot opt out of managing pupil behaviour. The question is how effectively we do it. We are all aware that classes where control is achieved through hostility and negative feedback will not be environments conducive to learning. The management style we use can increase behavioural problems or reduce them. How we manage classroom activities will also help or hinder.

Do we 'manage by walkabout'?

Teachers exert a huge degree of influence on the behaviour of their pupils by their movement about the classroom and the eye contact they give the pupils. This is often referred to as proximity control.

Do pupils know the rules that are operating in their class?

The classroom ground-rules should be displayed for all pupils to see and should be communicated clearly to the parents through school brochures.

Do we comment on appropriate behaviour or just the problem behaviour?

Do we keep calm and treat behavioural difficulties or do we personalise such behaviour by attributing negative personality traits? Such an approach will more often generate more resentment and hostility.

Do we put pupils into situations where they are faced by a 'win-lose' situation?

It will be less likely for the pupils' long-term commitment to the classroom and school if they are regularly disempowered by confrontations in which the odds are stacked against them. Such an approach will often tend to escalate the degree of confrontation.

Teacher-Centred Difficulties

Individual teachers do make an enormous difference. They can convey a 'can do' feeling amongst all of their pupils when they are feeling well and 'on top of things'. Sadly, when they are under strain, teachers can inadvertently convey a very different message to their pupils. The increased stressors on teachers are well recognised. We cannot ignore the fact that many children are coming into learning environments lacking the necessary basic social skills etc. When schools reflected the home philosophy of punitive measures to control children, there were 'apparently' fewer problems in schools. Schools have changed dramatically – for the better – in this respect. Their approach to learning, actively involving pupils, democratises school to a greater extent. The majority of pupils have responded well to this transition but we are faced with some children who present adjustment difficulties within school environments. These can result in increased challenges for all teachers.

There are times in the teacher's life (as any other professional's) when they are more vulnerable to stress than others. One of the features of effective schools is that they recognise these times and offer support to colleagues when it is needed. Holmes and Rahe (1967) identified a taxonomy of these difficulties. Of course, different people can cope with stress in different ways. Some can handle significant stressors with apparent ease, others need the support of their colleagues and family more readily. The following table rates life events from the more serious to the less serious. Holmes and Rahe identified 43 different significant life events. We have listed the 15 most serious of those. The message is that at times when a number of these events come together to affect the individual they may be more vulnerable:

1. Death of a spouse
2. Divorce
3. Marital separation
4. Jail term
5. Death of a close family member
6. Personal injury or illness
7. Marriage
8. Loss of job
9. Marital reconciliation
10. Retirement
11. Change in health of family member
12. Pregnancy
13. Sexual problems
14. Arrival of new family member
15. Organisational readjustment

We have included in this book some ideas on managing stress because

• children with EBD are a significant source of stress for teachers;

• children with EBD suffer most when their teacher is stressed (see Appendix 3).

Within Pupil

Children can be under pressure just as schools and adults. This pressure may be of expectation placed on them by home and school. They have worries to do with friends or experience pressure of their reactions to home difficulties. Each of these will mean that at times we will be teaching children who are under considerable stress, and just like us they have to cope with it somehow.

Some will act out. They become very sensitive to criticism, just like adults. They may displace their aggressive feelings onto others. Others may act in. They may withdraw, and become depressed or apathetic. Such behaviours reflect inner difficulties. Evidence exists (Rutter et al) that indicates that children who face such life stresses as family bereavement, serious illness, parental separation, new family members, experience more problems in school, have more peer relationship difficulties and a lower frustration tolerance as well as conduct difficulties.

The child may have a medical condition or syndrome which affects their behaviour e.g. Autism, Asperger Syndrome, Tourettes Syndrome. Childhood cancer could also be an antecedent to a significant loss of motivation or energy. The Contact A Family (CAF) Directory (see list of helpful organisations) lists a wide range of such conditions and give details of possible prognoses and support groups which may offer advice to parents or professionals.

Formalising Concerns

All of the above behaviours or more pertinently a combination of them, evident in a number of school settings, could constitute a problem that should be responded to by the school at Stage 2 or 3 of the *Code of Practice* recommendations. The degree to which any child is showing emotional and behavioural difficulties will depend on the following dimensions:

1. the seriousness of the behaviour causing concern;
2. the rationality of the behaviour;
3. the predictability of the behaviour;
4. the longevity of the behaviour;
5. the resistance to change of the behaviour;
6. the absence of alternative explanations for the behaviour.

The above presents the teacher with a considerable dilemma. Given the large number of variables which impact on a child's behaviour, how can they effect change when they have concerns? How is the teacher able to be objective and systematic? How can this be reconciled with the need to react with urgency that is sometimes required with EBD? How can teachers be sensitive to the interactive nature of behavioural problems?

Gathering Evidence

Much of the evidence relating to children with complex difficulties will be contained in the records gained from monitoring of behavioural programmes that have been used. In the early stages it is important to be systematic in detailing concerns and recording the outcome of different interventions. One way of ensuring that decisions about behaviour are based on evidence is to keep a log of the child's behaviour. This is an extremely helpful thing to do but has the following drawbacks:

- it can be very time-consuming for the teacher;

- it does not address frustrations which may be the cause of the child's difficulties;

- the information it provides may be non-specific if careful thought is not given about what behaviours to record.

This can present substantial difficulties. All too often the outcome is too heavy a focus on negative behaviours. By compiling a log of incidents it is easy to fall into the trap of gathering lists of misdemeanors of the child. Inevitably the number of recorded incidents will be increased by the fact that the child is being closely observed. There will be less leeway for those things the child 'gets away with' under normal circumstances, a factor that many children rely on in schools to maintain their equilibrium.

Some children may seek attention by presenting those very behaviours that the teacher is concerned about once they know they are being recorded. Imagine the range of behaviours that children show in front of a camera. (Watching some breakfast TV can be a revelation about the way children and some adults behave in this respect.) Are those behaviours likely to be representative of the child's general behaviour?

Recording behaviour through log books can be fraught with difficulties and can result in very unpredictable outcomes. One example would be where a child presents a high degree of off-task interfering behaviour. If the class teacher responds to this by diligently recording every misdemeanor that the child commits over a period of two weeks, at the end of that time they could have a dossier amounting to many pages. How helpful is that information?

- Does it say the child behaves badly?

- Does it say the child is poorly stimulated and badly managed?

- Does it say anything about the exceptions to misbehaviour?

Those exceptions may be an important element of the foundations upon which a behavioural programme will be established. The behaviour log does nothing directly to change the behaviour causing concern. If that behaviour is severely affecting other children then it cannot be allowed to continue while behaviour logs are compiled.

Behaviour logs can show the incidence of specific behaviours but their wider use needs to be approached cautiously. Compiling a behaviour log will be a useful project to establish a baseline from which progress will be monitored. It is also a useful part of the monitoring process once a behavioural programme has been established.

It is helpful in addition to behaviour logs to record a broader range of data in relation to a teacher's concern. It must be stressed that we are not arguing for even more data to be gathered but that a different type of data be assembled. Quality of information in this issue is much more important than quantity. When gathering data it is important to look for triggers to behaviour, patterns of behaviour, areas of emerging behaviour, exceptions to problem behaviour, areas of strength in the child or group.

Observations

Before deciding on the type of behavioural techniques to be used to respond to a child's behaviour we must decide how we intend observing and recording. This is very important because it helps us better understand the difficulty and it can also help us, at a later stage, to see if our interventions are working. Without careful observations we may miss small improvements. People understandably want a problem behaviour to stop once some programme of intervention has been introduced. This is rarely the case. In fact, the behaviour may even get worse at first. Whatever the reasons for a child feeling and behaving as they do, it is helping them obtain something they need, e.g.:

- If they crave adult attention, playing the fool in class achieves this.

- If they crave kindness and encouragement, being withdrawn and depressed may achieve this.

By the time we are formalising our concerns, behaviour has usually become well entrenched. We will need patience and commitment to change matters. Without carefully observed information we will be less likely to notice the small improvements.

It is important to record behaviour in a systematic manner. You will need to consider the following areas:

Learning: on/off task behaviour; (see Appendix 1) targets set and achieved; tests results;

Pupil interactions: time spent with peers, activities engaged in;

Teacher-pupil   number of positive/negative communications, nature of interaction;
interactions:

Pupil behaviour: in/out of seat; specific behavioural concern, fighting, shouting out of class, running away.

Data should reflect the action the school has taken to help the child overcome the 'problem' behaviour and the response of the child to those interventions. Section 3:69 of the *Code of Practice* details the further evidence that the school should seek. This is discussed further in Chapter 6 Statutory Assessment.

Designing Behaviour Programmes

The best way to change children's behaviour is to change what you are doing.

When setting up a behavioural programme *always* include some measure of learning and one or two of the other areas as indicators of improvement.

Remember you need to be able to show even small improvements.

To make a judgment about a child presenting emotional and behavioural difficulties the class teacher or SENCO should go through a process which establishes:

- a clear description of the behaviour causing concern;

- the frequency of that behaviour;

- a programme aimed to reduce that behaviour (this will take the form of an individual education plan (IEP). See the discussion and examples in Chapter 4;

- a clear description of the indicators which will show that things are improving;

- monitoring of changes to or persistence of the behaviour;

- some description of the outcome (evaluation) of that programme.

Decisions about whether a child has emotional and behavioural difficulties should come at the end of an action learning cycle which is referred to in greater detail later on but which can be seen in the following model. *Figure 4* shows the four stages of the cycle as specified by the *Code of Practice* 3:69.

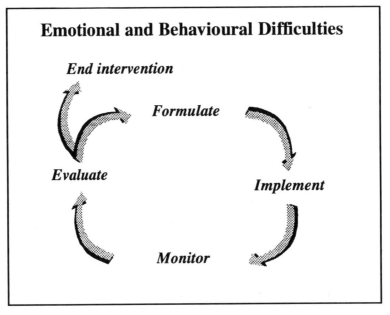

Figure 4 – The Emotional and Behavioural Difficulties Action Learning Cycle

Formulating Plans

At the formulation stage teachers, SENCOs and head teacher in liaison with parents must come to a decision about the level of response they intend to make to a child's difficulty. If the results of the behaviour are so problematic it is possible to provide the child directly with Stage 3 support or even refer directly to Stage 4 (Statutory Assessment). When increasing the level of support a child receives, whether that decision comes after a period of support at Stage 2 or directly in response to serious concerns, the school should consult with external professionals.

Contingency Planning

Teachers will always face dilemmas about the appropriateness of the response they give to behavioural difficulties. The prospect of overreacting to difficulties seems to trouble teachers as much as the possibility of under-reacting. One way of providing a sense of security in the face of such dilemmas is to establish contingency plans at the point of formulation. A contingency plan is an agreed 'what if?' response to a 'worst scene' development.

Use of a contingency plan can be illustrated through a short case study.

Case Study: Darren

Darren's behaviour presented a number of concerns:

- he was very distractible in the classroom;

- when the teacher intervened Darren engaged her in seemingly interminable debates about the appropriateness of the rules she was imposing and whether she was even-handed in applying the rules;

- he often roamed around the classroom when restless;

- he destroyed his own and other children's work;

- he hit other children.

A programme was devised using the 'Lesson Behaviour Monitoring Sheets' which are included in Appendix 4. In drawing up the plan it was decided that three elements of Darren's behaviour should be regarded as unacceptable in the classroom:

- sustained debates with the teacher disturbed the work of other children and therefore at a time to be decided by the teacher Darren was to be given two clear warnings that he must settle down and get on with his work. If he continued to argue after the second warning the contingency plan was to be implemented;

- destroying other children's work was unacceptable and would be responded to with the contingency plan;

- hitting other children was equally unacceptable and would result in use of the contingency plan.

The contingency plan consisted of Darren leaving the classroom for the duration of the lesson and going quietly to work in the classroom next door. If Darren resisted this move, refused to comply or disturbed the work of the other pupils in the receiving class he would then be told to report to the head teacher. If he resorted to aggressive behaviour then he would be excluded from school for the rest of the day. Darren's mother agreed that at this point she would call in to school to collect him.

Such a plan can be easily escalated and there is potential for the child to become a victim in the process. On the other hand sustaining unacceptable behaviour in the classroom is equally problematic for the child concerned or other pupils. To overcome the possible harmful effects of a contingency plan the following considerations should apply:

- the work given to the child must be appropriate;

- the rules of the classroom must be clearly communicated to the child;

- there should be a strong emphasis on building through positive action rather than control through sanctions;

- individual achievements, appropriate for their abilities, should be sought for all children;

- individual achievements should be celebrated continuously with small symbolic celebrations;

- behavioural progress from the child should be acknowledged by the teacher;

- the use of the contingency plan must be discussed with and agreed to by the child and their parents;

- the child should be listened to and concerns they may have should be addressed;

- use of the contingency plan should be seen as a limited period intervention;

- if the contingency plan is used regularly (once a day is certainly too often) then it should be renegotiated.

Not all behavioural programmes need a contingency plan. They are most effective when responding to those pupils who have conduct disorders, who are acting out, and behaving in challenging/disruptive ways. The *Figure 4* action learning cycle model for such pupils will be modified as in *Figure 5*.

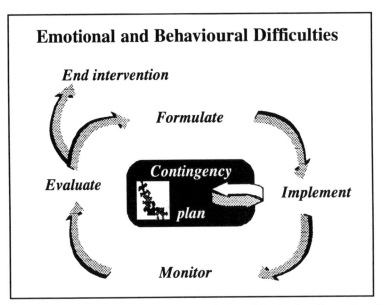

Figure 5 – An augmented version of the EBD Action Learning Cycle

Why do difficulties often persist even when the original cause for them has been removed?

We can all think of pupils whose behaviour improved incredibly quickly following our intervention and others who seemed as bad no matter what we did. This resistance to behavioural improvements can be illustrated through a further case study.

Case Study: Paul

- He is aggressive and challenging to certain teachers and almost on the edge of more serious disciplinary problems.

- His parents rarely attend school.

- Paul struggles with his work and has a hostile, defiant attitude to help of any kind.

- Paul has experienced the most inconsistent care and control from adults that you could imagine.

- Now you introduce a new programme, perhaps consulting with an educational psychologist, in designing the strategy.

- Paul's behaviour is extremely resistant to change.

He has learnt through experience that this 'new consistency programme' will pass, just as all the others have. His maladaptive behaviour is the result of a series of interconnected long-term problems. It is difficult to isolate any single stressor and so the maladaptive behaviour continues for some time despite the programme.

REMEMBER when you set up interventions that you believe are in a pupil's best interests then keep doing them. If you are in charge of the programme, expect little initial improvements and that any immediate improvements may be short-lived. New attempts need to be given a fair chance to work. It will be helpful to identify slight improvements within the first few weeks but it will more likely be several months before significant improvements are evident although it is again important to stress that hard and fast rules are very often broken. The process of change will most likely be slow and often erratic – 'two steps forward and one step backwards'.

Be concerned during the early days with the way your interventions are being carried out. Take time to reassure, praise and support those who are closely involved. The best way to identify those early improvements is to have good clear data on the incidence of those behaviours which worry you. Careful collection of data before and during the programme will prove invaluable.

Clearly we can never know all of the influences on a child. There are times when children face distresses that they cannot manage, and feel they have no one to confide in. Imagine a pupil who is experiencing cruel bullying in school.

- They feel unable to tell anyone at home because of family difficulties.

- In school they feel they 'must not' violate the rule of 'not telling on others'.

- Worry and anxiety affects their behaviour, and their attitude to work.

- Teachers know something is going on but feel unable to get to the bottom of it.

- When it finally comes out into the open, matters are resolved and a marked improvement in the pupil is quickly seen.

The pupil's maladaptive behaviour changes when the stressor which is causing it is removed. The stressor unfortunately is not always easily identified.

Gains and Losses in Problem Behaviour

Often a child presenting behavioural difficulties is sustained by the short-term gains their problem behaviours bring. Alternatively teachers are motivated by the knowledge that short-term gains must be balanced against long-term losses. (See *Figure 6*.) Sometimes it is helpful to explore the motivators in a problem behaviour from the pupil's perspective in order to understand the issue of resistance to change.

SHORT-TERM GAINS A pupil's behaviour will be resistant to change because of the short-term gains it produces.	LONG-TERM LOSSES In the long-term, however, there are many losses.
predictable and manageable negative relationship with adults (this is what pupil is used to)	poor academic attainments
avoidance of difficult work	negative self-image: 'I'm thick', 'I'm a troublemaker'
excitement of conflict	poor relationships skills with adults
peer kudos	peer rejection
revenge	
release of aggressive feelings	

Figure 6

Working in Partnership with Parents

Establishing effective partnership with parents presents a varied set of challenges and opportunities in relation to EBD. The sensitivity of the issue is discussed in section 2.29 of the *Code of Practice*: '...*parents may feel they are being blamed for their child's difficulties when the school first raises questions with them...*' Parents may feel two strong emotions in relation to this. Firstly they will feel a sense of insecurity: their child is being criticised and the instant reaction is to jump to the defence of the child which can make them feel in opposition to the school. The second feeling may be of inadequacy. The parent may have struggled long and hard with the child and feel as though the school is passing its responsibility for solving the difficulties on to them, where they feel at their wits' end. Parents may feel very vulnerable in such circumstances.

The importance of the parents' role is emphasised in the *Code of Practice* section 2.30: '*If a child has a behavioural difficulty, or is following a developmental activity of any kind which requires a structured approach in school, reinforcement at home by parents will be crucial.*' Entering into a joint problem solving relationship with parents, at as early a stage as possible, listening carefully to their concerns and agreeing on mutual targets is likely to bring the best possible results. *Circular 9/94* makes this point: *'It is important to do everything possible to establish early working relationships with parents. Parents may bring about significant changes in their child's behaviour. Teachers should avoid prejudging parents' abilities to respond. In some cases co-operation will not be forthcoming and schools will need to use their best endeavours without it.'*

In order to sustain positive relationships with parents it is helpful to remind yourself of some guidelines before each contact with them. It is always worth remembering for the parent it is never easy to go into a school to discuss their child's progress. Where behaviour difficulties have been identified it is even more difficult.

Meetings With Parents: Making Them Work

Do:
- meet with the parents in a setting which is comfortable and quiet and free from interruptions;

- try wherever possible to get another member of staff or volunteer to look after their young children during your meeting (young children and adults meeting to solve complex problems are not usually a good mix. The end result is the parent becomes increasingly anxious and that is not helpful);

- make sure that the parent is aware that you appreciate/recognise their child's strengths and qualities;

- spend time establishing small achievable targets;

- talk positively about the child in front of their parent/carer;

- make sure you set targets that are small and achievable, to give a sense of early success;

- show understanding of the difficulties that the parent may be experiencing at home;

- acknowledge that children with such difficulties usually do improve when a plan of action is agreed;

- make time to explain your objectives and involve the parent in setting targets for the child's IEP;

- stress that it is the child's behaviour that is a cause for concern, not the child;

- fix regular follow-up meetings where necessary;

- plan ahead to identify ways of coping with the most difficult behaviour, avoiding crisis responses;

- praise and show appreciation for their efforts and support (parents with a low self-esteem will be less effective in support);

- make sure you finish a meeting having given the parent a sense of their child being valued and of the parent's support being really needed;

- record all parental meetings and any agreements or action points in the child's case history or SEN file.

Don't:
- use threats as a way of managing the problem, 'and unless they improve we will be forced to...';

- hold intimidating meetings with large numbers of professionals;

- hand out a lot of reports etc. at meetings which the parents have not had a chance to see before;

- let parents be put off if their child's behaviour gets worse when any plan is tried;

- use excessive jargon;

- allow children to become labelled as 'disruptive', 'naughty';

- get trapped into only talking about the 'problem' behaviour;

- go looking for 'blame';

- use simple 'media type' explanations for complicated and multi-causal behaviour;

- promise things that you cannot deliver;

- be intimidated or lose your cool (calm assertive behaviour will enable constructive relationships to be sustained);

- prolong meetings that are beginning to be fuelled by anger and resentment (arrange another meeting with support);

- collude with one parent's negative views about their partner, the child or your colleagues.

The Pupil's Perspective

One significant area of contention during the consultation period before the publication of the *Code of Practice* related to the conferring with pupils. Unlike the *Children Act 1989*, the *Education Act 1993* places no legal obligation to consult with a pupil about their SEN plans. There is, however, encouragement to involve pupils as much as possible in the decisions that are made about their education. Problem behaviour is often an expression of deep anxiety, frustration and powerlessness on the part of the child. Any programme which fails to address those strong feelings is likely to be unsuccessful. See Appendix 6 The Pupil Planner for a helpful way of finding more about their perceptions, and involving the pupil drawing up their programmes or individual education plans. Programmes which are established *with* the child are more likely to engender a sense of ownership and responsibility in them than those that are done *to* them. *Circular 9/94* supports this view:

Pupils should be encouraged to set and organise learning goals for themselves; monitor their own progress; reflect on their learning, personal and social situations; describe their preferred tasks and work areas; and work cooperatively with their peers. They should be encouraged to participate directly in the compilation of records of achievement.

Listening to children with emotional and behavioural difficulties

There is no blue print which will ensure that every meeting we have with a troubled child is successful. But there are guidelines which come from the many professionals and skilled helpers who work in this area. While it can never be a science, we can make efforts to increase our success. There will be occasions when we say the 'wrong thing' or face a wall of silence. We can only learn through having the commitment to make 'virtuous mistakes'.

The ideas presented below are by no means all-inclusive. Each teacher will develop a style which works for them. For the newcomer the prospect of interviewing a pupil with emotional and behavioural difficulties may seem daunting. The ideas presented below are an attempt to show that through reflection and practice we can develop/improve the necessary skills. The age and maturity of the child will always be an important factor to take into account.

Listening skills

Our aim in listening to pupils should be to enable them to feel heard and understood. Try to encourage them to 'teach you' about who they are. Ask for clarification if you do not understand. Avoid interrogating them 'to get to the bottom' of their troubles. This will teach them to be passive and just answer your questions. You may find asking closed/factual questions can help put a pupil at ease. You can then move on to more open-ended questions, such as 'Tell me about what happened at lunch time?' Keep asking yourself, 'Do I understand what is being said?' If the answer is 'No', then be prepared to ask for further information/clarification.

Listening style

The nature of emotional and behavioural difficulties is that such children are used to being rejected. Aim to maintain a relaxed body posture and an unhurried gentle tone of voice. Use verbal and non-verbal assurances to support their efforts to talk. Show genuine interest.

The setting

If you are meeting with a pupil alone in a room, allow them to sit nearest the door, perhaps leaving the door slightly ajar. Do not sit directly opposite them, which can make eye contact challenging. Sit at an angle to them so that their natural eye gaze is not towards you. If you have 30 minutes to talk with them, tell them at the start of your interview. When you only have five minutes left, tell them. Avoid asking them if they understand; instead ask them to tell you what it is that has been said or agreed etc. At the end of the meeting ask them for the key points that have emerged.

Leverage points

There can often be some aspect in a situation that is causing a pupil particular concern. It may be their relationships with their family, friends, teacher or other involved adult. Such concern/pain can be a good motivation to try to improve matters. We can often focus on those issues that concern us rather than the pupil. It is always good to try to ensure that any IEP has built-in success. Look for small goals or leverage ones that genuinely motivate.

Confidentiality

It is not uncommon for some of the difficulties children face to stem from problem relationships and they may ask you not to tell anyone else. The pupil may feel that they are betraying a friend or adult. If the information given by the child indicates that they or someone else is in danger, then it is your responsibility to inform your head teacher and other relevant agencies. While you may feel that you are breaking their confidence, the safety of the young person or another person's safety must be paramount. The following information can helpfully convey your continuing care and support for the pupil under such circumstances.

'Ordinarily what is said in these meetings is private and between you and me only. This means that we won't gossip to people who don't need to know. But if something is said – which means that "you" or somebody else is in some sort of danger, and needs protecting – then I will speak to those people who need to know. I will explain to you who I will have to see and why. I will keep working with you on this problem until you feel that things are OK.'

Maintaining a professional distance

There can be occasions in a relationship developing between you and a pupil when you feel that they are becoming over-dependent, even too personal. Under such circumstances it can help to meet with the pupil only with a third party, preferably a colleague. This can safely alter the dynamics of the 'me and you' relationship.

Coping with silence

We will all meet the reluctant or resistant pupil. Most of us find silence difficult to manage. We can feel that we must fill the gap at all costs. We need to differentiate between silences, and respond accordingly. There are many types of silence:

- thought;

- confusion;

- uncertainty;

- resistance;

- protection;

- trauma.

Emotionally volatile children

When the pupil's difficulty is in response to internal emotions, anger or grief for example, then such children may suddenly express strong emotions. We may have little warning or insight as to the trigger. Unless the child is in danger of harming themselves or others, try to contain the emotions until the child is calm and in need of comfort and reassurance. At such times children can be very frightened of their intense feelings. Remember children have the same feelings of sadness and anger as adults. Thankfully they seem to have a 'shorter sadness span'. Children may wonder if what they are experiencing is normal.

Empathising

Sometimes the way to appreciate the emotions a child is feeling is through putting yourself in their place. Become a method actor. If you were them, what feelings would your behaviour indicate – anger, sadness, rejection? What feelings do they seem to stir up in you? These may well be the very feelings that they are experiencing.

Problem-free talk

Be careful not to over-focus on the problem. Find out what interests the pupil, what skills and qualities they have. It is these that will support them through this difficult time. Search for exceptions from the problem: 'When was the last time that you felt at ease in your class group? What was different about that time from the other times when you feel unhappy?'

Self-esteem

End your meeting by focusing on those aspects that set a positive tone. Set targets that the pupil will be able to achieve. Give them coping strategies to deal with difficult situations and feelings. Restate your commitment to continue to support them.

Child Protection

When faced with a child presenting serious or persistent behaviour difficulties, teachers often ask, 'What have I done wrong?' Sometimes it is necessary for the teacher to ask, 'What are others doing wrong to cause this child's problems?' As we have already pointed out, it is all too easy to get into the blame game. We believe that in ordinary circumstances, fault and blame offer unhelpful explanations and should be avoided. Such questions, however, need to be considered if you suspect that anybody has done or intends to do something, with the expected result being some harm, or potential harm to the child's well-being or development.

Sadly for some children the stressor at the root of their EBD will be abuse. If you become concerned that a child in your care is being abused through evidence of:

- non-accidental injury;

- excessive punishments;

- disclosure of sexual abuse, directly to you, through other children in school, or because of sudden changes in the child's behaviour e.g. inappropriate sexual behaviour;

- indications of neglect in their clothes or hygiene;

- emotional abuse shown in mood swings, tearfulness etc.;

it is essential that you discuss your concerns with your head teacher. Where concerns exist the *Child Protection Procedures*, which must be produced by local authorities, should be followed. The first point of contact is the duty social worker in the child's neighbourhood patch office.

If in doubt, make a referral.

Child and Adolescent Mental Health

At the extreme end of the EBD continuum are those who can be described as having childhood mental illness. It is rare for children to be described as mentally ill. This is mostly because mental illness is usually evaluated in terms of the interference it causes with the individual's ability to sustain normal relationships and to live independently. These children are supported by adults so much that making judgments about the likelihood of a mental illness interfering with the individual ability to live independently is neither helpful nor desirable.

Using the same parameters of seriousness and duration of behaviour, there are some children who are given that label. As children enter adolescence, more mental illnesses are identified with the greater incidence of:

- eating disorders;

- phobias;

- obsessive compulsive disorders;

- substance misuse;

- depression;

- attempted suicide.

Responsibility for mental health services lies with the Health Authorities (the Child and Adolescent Mental Health Services, CAMHS) and Social Services departments. The following definition is contained in *Circular 9/94*:

Disorders or illnesses are rare in children and young people, and may be episodic, but are generally indicated by significant changes in behaviour, emotions, or thought processes which are so prolonged and/or so severe that, taking into account the child's development and the socio-cultural context, they interfere profoundly with everyday life and are a serious disability for the child, the family, friends or those who care for or teach the child.

Advice on the strategies for responding to mental health issues with children and young people is contained in *A Handbook on Child and Adolescent Mental Health* published jointly by the Departments for Education and Employment and Health. It discusses a number of themes for action:

- multi-agency needs assessment;

- matching available resources to local needs;

- setting planning priorities;

- developing contracts for child and adolescent mental health services;

- strengthening specialist services;

- co-operating with other purchasers to ensure the consistent provision of more specialist services;

- operating within multi-disciplinary specialist services and linking with non-specialist and other specialist services.

Summary

Emotional and behavioural difficulties, like other areas of SEN, can be seen on a continuum. There are a number of features of EBD that make them different from other areas of special educational need:

- difficulties in reaching clear definitions of EBD;

- the impact they have on teachers and other pupils;

- the possibility of hidden stressors as causation;

- the need for a trial and error approach initially;

- the potential for resistance to change.

Like other areas of special educational needs, the solutions are as much about adjusting programmes of study to enable the child to succeed as they are about changing the child. Unlike many other areas of special educational needs the prospect of a complete recovery is always present. The child who is 'just like any other child only more so' can, with sensitive support, become 'just like any other child'.

Chapter 3 – Strategies: Code of Practice Stage 1

Managing Emotional and Behavioural Difficulties

However interesting, plausible and appealing a theory may be, it is techniques, not theories, that are actually used on people.

London, P (1964)

Beyond understanding the nature of the difficulties (the theory), teachers need to ask: 'What can be done within the framework of the *Code of Practice* to support pupils with emotional and behavioural difficulties?'

At Stage 1 the class teacher needs to ask the right questions. The 'Registering a Concern' questionnaire may prove useful in asking key questions (see *Figure 7*). (This may be photocopied as an *aide-mémoire* if it is helpful to you.)

Teacher/Curriculum Focus

Some children present difficulties despite the most efficient classroom management by the teacher. It is helpful therefore to have a number of well-tried techniques upon which to base programmes for these pupils.

Chapter 2 illustrated that many of the causes of emotional and behavioural difficulties will lie outside of our control and will even be outside of our understanding. It is not helpful, however, to worry greatly about this. The explanations for children's behaviour are varied and complex. Many different ways of making sense of them exist, and they are each possible and conceivably appropriate. What really matters is what suggestions such explanations give us, and can we use them within the school context?

A theory which results in intensive 1:1 therapy will have little application in a mainstream school. It is no less valid than the theory which recommends planned ignoring or a systematic approach to reward and sanctions. It is just that the latter can be tried out much more readily in the context of the ordinary classroom.

Worrying about those things that you have little or no control over, will probably increase your own stress. A good teacher will always make a difference and will be even more effective where they can refer to a range of techniques to use as 'special measures'.

• Do not worry about things that you cannot do anything about.

• Do not worry about those things that you can do something about.

The first task in responding to a behavioural difficulty is to review all of the features of your current classroom practice to see if there are aspects of what you currently do which can be emphasised or adapted to meet the child's needs.

Have you:
• matched work to the pupil's ability (differentiation)?

The most helpful of first line strategies is to consider that the pupil's behaviour difficulties are a reaction to work which is too difficult for them.

• increased the menu of rewards?

for work completed or evidence of efforts in relation to those behaviours causing concern e.g. getting on better with the other pupils, increased on-seat behaviour, increased task-focused behaviour?

• developed a menu of short-term rewards?

Make sure pupils receive rewards early in the classroom process. Divide the day into chunks. Many pupils may find it difficult to work for long-term rewards.

• actively involved the pupil in target setting and rewards?

Negotiate reasonable targets for pupils to work towards. Pupils will often work harder towards targets that they have identified. Negotiating rewards often helps to make the reward more meaningful to the pupil. A simple ten-minute counselling-style session can often help (see *Figure 8*). Also see Appendix 2 The Personal Improvement Plan.

Pupil Behaviour Registering a Concern: Initial Overview		
Pupil's Name _____ D.O.B. ___/___/___ Yr. Grp _____		

Who does this pupil's behaviour worry? ....

Is the pupil aware of my concerns? ....   Yes   No

With which teachers/lessons does the child present similar difficulties?

....

Have I informed other key teachers? ....   Yes   No

Are there home difficulties? ....   Yes   No

Does the pupil have any medical/physical problems? ....   Yes   No

Are there community difficulties (neighbour disputes etc.)? ....   Yes   No

Do other pupils react negatively with this pupil? ....   Yes   No

Is the pupil being bullied? ....   Yes   No

Have I identified and built on this pupil's strengths? ....   Yes   No

Does the pupil have learning difficulties? ....   Yes   No

Behaviours giving me concern?

What? ....

When? ....

Where? ....

With whom? ....

How often? ....

Have I identified what happens before, during and after the problem
behaviour? (Antecedents Behaviour Consequences) ....   Yes   No

Do I have a record of what has already been tried? Was it effective?   Yes   No
If it was ineffective, why do you think it didn't work?

Do I need to start some form of recording measure: book or card?   Yes   No

Teacher's Name _____   **Date** ___/___/___

Figure 7

Step 1
Discuss your concerns with the pupils. Wherever possible encourage the pupil to identify those behaviours which you consider to be a problem.

Step 2
Agree on the nature of your concern or those concerns which have been reported to you.

Step 3
Elicit from the pupil actions they may take to reduce the concern. Discuss the merits of suggestions made but try not to be too interventionist. The aim of this part of the process is to help the pupil to take responsibility for their behaviour.

Step 4
Agree on two or three targets arising from the conversation and agree to meet next week to see how the pupil is progressing with their agreed objectives.

This formalised procedure should be noted down and the pupil reminded in subsequent sessions of the targets they set for themselves. An example of a recording procedure for this is in Appendix 6.

Figure 8

- related teaching to pupils' interests?

A pupil may have out-of-school interests which can be used to make learning more relevant. The film *Kes* gives a perfect illustration of this although sadly it did not result in a positive outcome in that story.

- varied your teaching style?

Pupils have different styles of learning. There is some evidence to suggest that learning and/or behaviour difficulties emerge when the teacher's instructional style is markedly different from the pupil's learning style.

- explained the learning goals to the pupils?

It is always worth discussing the new skills and knowledge that the pupils will gain from a given task. When they are 'let in on the secret' they can work towards common goals with their teacher.

Do you:
- build the pupils' self-esteem?

Confident pupils learn better and have less need to mask their difficulties with work avoidance or disruptive behaviours. Help them to recognise their skills and personal qualities. Help them to feel valued and to value each other.

- use open-ended questioning?

Closed questions require little feedback and limit interaction. Asking open-ended questions e.g. 'tell me what you were expecting to happen when you...' conveys a sense of trust in the pupils that their answers are of importance.

- focus on behaviour, not pupil?

Whenever unhelpful, inappropriate or unacceptable behaviour occurs the message that should be given to the pupils is that they are still OK in your eyes. It is the behaviour which you are bothered about. By adopting such a strategy it is easier to enlist the pupil's help in overcoming the difficulty.

- use humour sensitively?

Sensitive humour can take the edge off painful situations and enable people to gather their resources to tackle the problem. *By the same token insensitive humour, especially sarcasm, can be a destructive force and can set up barriers between people.*

• remain calm but firm?

Body language, tone of voice and general demeanour communicate to the pupils as much as what you say. The message to the pupils should be 'I am very concerned about this situation and I will manage it effectively, even if that entails seeking support from one of my colleagues.'

• praise your pupils in front of other teachers?

A helpful demonstration of the value you place on your pupils is that you relate their successes publicly to your colleagues. It also reinforces in the pupil's eyes that teachers get pleasure from their pupils' achievements. Pupils can be sent, with prior agreement, to colleagues for rewards. In this way you make the process ceremonial and thus more meaningful and memorable.

• use other teachers to support you?

Develop a team approach to behavioural concerns. (See Chapter 7 on whole school approaches.)

• catch pupils doing well and reward?

Rewarding spontaneously occurring behaviour which is consistent with the targets you have set can be a very effective motivator for the pupil. Try this approach taken from *Solution Focused Brief Therapy* (Fogell 1996):

1. You have a pupil causing concern.

2. Imagine a miracle happened one night while everyone was asleep and the problem disappeared.

3. What would be different about the child the following day? Make a list of the five most important changes in their behaviour (indicators) which would tell you the problem had lessened or even disappeared.

4. For the next few weeks watch out for circumstances in which the child is showing behaviour close to those five indicators.

5. Reward those spontaneously occurring behaviours, discussing them with the pupil and celebrating progress in your usual way.

• express disappointment at problem behaviour?

Expressing disappointment rather than anger or frustration communicates to the child that you believe they are capable of controlling their behaviour. A show of genuine surprise at their misbehaviour can be a statement of confidence in them generally.

Have you:
• varied group work?

Where there are a range of activities in the classroom, it is important to communicate to the child their explicit learning and behavioural goals. The aim will be to give the children opportunities to learn independently not the opportunity to opt out.

• made learning interesting and fun?

Pupils learn best when they are confident and happy. Often poor behaviour occurs when the subject matter is confusing or heavy going. It can help at such times to reinforce the work by the use of games, quizzes, audio-visual presentations, visiting speakers.

• used systematic praise and positive attention?

See the Rules Praise Ignore as a good example of this (Appendix 5).

• developed clear positive rules with pupils?

Involve the pupils in setting clear consistent ground rules. The 1 in 3 Programme is a good example of this (see *Figure 9*).

In our class we have a 1 into 3 rule

1:    **RESPECT** for

       SELF

3:    OTHERS

       PROPERTY

In PSE lessons each one of these is focused on for a day and positive ways of showing respect are discussed. The pupils' suggestions can then become the focus of written work, artwork, displays, plays, puppet shows etc.

Figure 9

• sought in-class support and advice?

Two or three heads can be better than one. It is important for the whole staff team that colleagues can talk openly about behaviour difficulties.

• developed organisational arrangement for diverting or diffusing problem situations?

If you anticipate difficulties with a particular pupil or group it can be a useful diversion to develop a team teaching approach or other joint activity.

• set up problem avoidance tasks?

e.g. If you have to divert attention to talk to a specific pupil, it helps if you can ask the rest of the group to please get on with a given task.

• developed a 'fire drill' for a behavioural emergency?

It is important that the pupils know very clearly what will happen if any behaviour 'seriously violates' the class rules. It is unfair to you and your pupils if confusion follows a serious incident. Having established your general classroom plans, you need to answer the 'what if ... happens?' question (see the section on contingency planning). Senior staff need to be included in developing such plans.

Do you:
• allow pupils to let off steam?

At times pupils may come in to school angry or agitated. These may be very appropriate feelings in response to difficult circumstances outside the classroom. Being angry is not a problem but the behaviour it leads to can be. Use selective activities to work through the feelings, e.g. ripping up paper to use in papier-mâché activities, scrubbing out paint pots. It is important that the pupils understand that this is a constructive gesture and not construed as making matters worse.

• have short-term targets and check pupils understand what is expected?

It is important that indicators of improvement are negotiated and the pupil understands the goals they have set for themselves. Once established these can help to encourage the teacher and pupil that progress is being made, or at worst a new approach is needed.

- convey an attitude of things are/will get better?

'Can do' attitudes are helpful when approaching behaviour difficulties. Start each day with a 'fresh start'. If behaviour gets better as a result of a self-fulfilling prophecy, that is good.

- send positive notes home?

Establish a principle that it is important to send more positive notes home than negative ones. It is particularly important to let parents know that the strategies you have devised are working. Often parents will be sceptical about the prospect of success. Positive notes home can be a big part in the process of whittling away at that scepticism.

- check room layout and use of resources?

Do you have blind spots in your classroom where misbehaviour starts? It is important that early into any behavioural programme, changes in furniture arrangements and seating plans are explored.

- manage by walking about?

Proximity control can be very effective in diverting potentially difficult behaviour. Make sure that you place yourself where you can give eye contact or gesture to as many pupils as possible.

- give responsibility tasks?

Have a range of 'high status' tasks which you can use to reward appropriate behaviour. You can project the status of the task. It is important, however, that the allocation of pupils to such tasks is monitored carefully.

- involve pupil in recording behaviour?

Ideally pupils will share with you a desire to make improvements. Where possible pupils should be encouraged to complete colourful or otherwise visually cheerful charts, which motivates them to make more progress.

- set up buddy systems?

Involving other pupils in supporting a child through a behavioural programme can be a very effective method of developing positive peer relationships. Programmes like the 'No Blame Approach' (Maines and Robinson, 1991) or 'circle time' are good examples of this.

- develop positive peer relationships?

Developing whole group activities through activities like 'circle time' which explore issues of assertiveness, feelings, fears, relationships in a safe environment can help to promote whole school values and can be a safety valve for less confident pupils.

Positive Classroom Management

The above strategies cannot be conducted in isolation. They will form part of an integrated complex pattern that is your classroom management. The way that you run your classroom will determine the style in which you implement individually differentiated behavioural responses. It is therefore important to consider the overall management of the classroom. The following ten ideas to reduce management problems are given with pedagogic justifications.

- Always expect the best from your pupils.

This shows that you have faith in them, and you believe that they can all behave well. Poor behaviour is always better seen as a departure from high expectations than as a confirmation of worst expectations.

- Make it clear what you expect from them.

Children without boundaries go in search of them. Establishing clear ground rules shows that you and your lessons are purposeful and you know the conditions that will help them learn. It helps to display conduct rules in the classroom, on corridors and in the dining hall. It also helps to discuss the behavioural expectations on the pupils. All too often behaviour is only discussed when the rules have been broken.

- Reward and praise them often.

This will enhance and strengthen their self-confidence. This is especially important when the class group is coping with disruptive and demanding behaviour. It will also model behaviour to the pupils that values positive appraisal and cooperative working. If teacher criticises less it is likely that the pupils will ...

- Involve your pupils in setting learning targets.

This will help to convey the message that the pupil is responsible for their own behaviour. It follows then that the teacher is confident in their ability to achieve change. In so doing it promotes independent learning.

- Value their efforts and achievements.

It is often easy to focus on the outcomes of behaviour programmes. In order to foster confidence it may be necessary to focus more on the processes and to recognise where efforts have been made. This is as true for the teacher as it is for the pupil. This will show them that effort and determination are valued qualities.

- Make time to get to know their personal qualities, interests and strengths.

This will show them that you value them as unique people. It increases the teacher's awareness of the possible areas to focus rewards.

- Avoid personalising problem behaviours.

Be hard on issues – caring towards pupils. This show the pupils that you value their right to learn and your right to teach. They will see that you believe pupils are OK, though their behaviour might need managing by both you and them.

- Explain your teaching aims at the start of lessons.

This will help pupils relate it to existing knowledge as well as being motivated to the new goal.

- Difficulties are an issue 'between' you and the pupil, not just 'in' them.

This shows your commitment to them and their learning. If they are not learning, you are not teaching.

- The best way to change a pupil's behaviour is to change what you do.

Classroom management is a skill. There are techniques that you can acquire. Every teacher will have been told at some time those short reminders on how to attain good discipline, e.g. Colin Smith, Lecturer at Birmingham University, described the four golden rules of classroom management:

1. Get 'em in
2. Get 'em at it
3. Keep 'em at it
4. Get 'em out

This may sound a little perfunctory or even militaristic. For the reflective teacher it can provide a useful basis for planning a lesson or, if things go badly, analysing the points of weakness at different stages of the lesson so that different approaches can be tried next time.

1. Get 'em in

Allows for consideration of the manner in which the teacher meets the pupils. Should they line up outside the classroom? Should they walk straight in and sit down? Which vulnerable pupils should be kept a close eye on? etc. In any problematic lesson, if that was the source of difficulties, how can the routines at the start of the lesson be adjusted to overcome difficulties?

2. Get 'em at it

Allows for consideration of the instructions given, access to resources, differentiation of materials or tasks for certain pupils, quality of the background information. If the pupils entered the lesson without difficulties and then problems occurred when the work was introduced, how can task presentation or demands be adjusted? Are there particular pupils for whom the teacher should direct their attention at this particular time?

3. Keep 'em at it

Alerts teachers to be sensitive to the group dynamics, the concentration levels of the pupils, the number of distractions allowed, the working environment for the pupils. If the pupils lose concentration easily, how can the task demands be adjusted? Are there unreasonable distractions in the lesson? How can adjustments be made?

4. Get 'em out

Alerts teacher to the issues around movement from one activity to another. Which pupils are vulnerable at that time? Are there any pupils who need an extra word of encouragement before they go? Have all of the pupils completed their tasks? Is the teacher able to ensure that the pupils move to their next activity in an orderly and controlled manner?

Careful analysis of the process of the lesson can be a very empowering experience for the class teacher. It enables problems to become points of learning and not inhibitors of teacher satisfaction.

The Sergeant-Major's Strategy

We are not suggesting the teacher adopts a pose of strutting about shouting offensively at anyone that moves (apologies to any offended sergeant-majors). At all points the teacher can vary the way they present material, the seating arrangements, the manner in which they approach the pupils. They can make changes and observe the effects.

The sergeant-major's strategy also helps to remind the busy teacher of the need to explain clearly what is expected.

An observer at a military display was so impressed with the precision with which the company of soldiers carried out their drill that he asked the sergeant-major how she managed to get such a level of co-operation from her soldiers.

'Well, sir,' she replied, *'Whenever I am telling them something important that they have to remember, I tell them what I'm about to tell them. Then I tell them. Then I tell them what I've told them.'*

If you have pupils who experience difficulties in adjusting to new activities or following simple instructions, the above approach can help the teacher to avoid unnecessary difficulties. It could also be enhanced by the teacher asking the pupil to repeat back instructions when they have been given to gauge the pupil's understanding of them.

Consequences

In general, the approaches we are recommending throughout this book lead to the view that punishment alone is an ineffective strategy. Instead it is usually more productive to teach pupils that there are consequences to what they do. These can be either positive or negative. To be most effective, consequences should follow as close in time to the child's behaviour as possible. The class teacher's aim should be to guide their pupils to be motivated to seek positive experiences but pupils should, as much as possible, be empowered to take responsibility for their own actions. The simple facts of consequences are:

- For something to be a positive consequence the pupil should be motivated to work towards obtaining it.

- For something to be a negative consequence they should work towards avoiding it.

A child's behaviour will be, to a large degree, determined by the consequences it achieves for them. If they do something which produces a pleasing outcome they are more likely to repeat that behaviour than if it produced an outcome they disliked. Class teachers should be aware of the different consequences of behaviour that are operating in their classroom and around school and observe how those consequences affect the pupils' behaviour. This will lead to an awareness that they can make adjustments to the range of positive and negative consequences.

In aiming to increase desired behaviours the class teacher will seek to follow the behaviour with positive consequences. What pupils value as positive consequences can be wide and varied and will, to a great extent, be dictated by the group. We all have different values whether individually or in groups. A positive consequence for the class teacher might be half an hour with feet up reading the Booker Prizewinner, but for many of the pupils that would be more like a chore.

If the class teacher wishes to decrease a certain behaviour, they would seek to follow it with negative consequences. Negative consequences are things which follow a child's behaviour which they are motivated to avoid; or when the removal of an event increases a certain behaviour. There will be times when we wish to use sanctions to decrease certain unacceptable behaviours. You will need to have a hierarchy of sanctions, from mild to increasing severity.

Matching the seriousness of a misdemeanor to the appropriateness of the punishment is very difficult at the best of times. Pupils with EBD magnify the difficulty often because their experience of punishment is likely to have been more erratic. Furthermore if a pupil repeats a negative behaviour after being 'told off' for it, there is a great temptation to move down to the next more severe sanction. This can result in a negative spiral from which it is difficult to escape. There will be some occasions when sanctions will be important and appropriate. Our message is that sanctions must be carefully planned when used, measured in their application, and thought likely, in the end, to achieve the desired outcome. (See Chapter 5 for the discussion on use of sanctions.) The teacher's aim is to find consequences which will motivate the pupil to change undesired behaviour and which are consistent with the ethos of the classroom and school.

Using Positive Reinforcement to Change Behaviour

Positive reinforcers such as praise are often used to increase specific desired behaviour. The withdrawal of positive rewards can also diminish unwanted behaviours. When planned ignoring of any low tariff inappropriate behaviour is used, it is often effective because of the removal of positive reinforcers for the pupil. Time out is such an example. (This is covered in more detail below.) In using positive reinforcers (rewards), the class teacher usually follows a process of:

STEP 1   Select the behaviour you wish to increase.

STEP 2   Discuss with the pupil the behaviour that is expected.

STEP 3   Based on knowledge of the pupil, set up positive and negative consequences for them working towards, or not, the set goal.

STEP 4   Obtain data as to how frequently the desired behaviour occurs.

STEP 5   Apply plan and monitor outcomes.

Types of positive reinforcers

The easiest and most effective positive reinforcement is teacher attention, praise and approval. But initially material rewards, activities etc. may be more effective.

Edible: sweets, crisps, fruit, drinks, raisins, nuts. (Be careful to involve/inform parents of the use of such rewards, a) they could be construed as bribery and b) in case children have an allergic reaction to certain foods, chocolate, nuts etc.)

Non-edible: balloons, toys, sport items, certificates, posters.

Activities: gym time, shop time, sport, trips, video.

Token: points for general exchange.

Social: attention, praise, work displayed, approval, privileges, special work, responsibilities.

Always aim to move from: *material* ➔ *token* ➔ *social*

Choosing rewards

Ask the pupil what they like. Observe if pupils ask for certain things. Do they seem to prefer certain activities over others? Will they work to obtain it?

Focusing on rewards can present dilemmas for all teachers. It is helpful to observe the following principles:

- Rewards should be available to all children in the class.

- Teacher should always remain in control of the issue of rewards or otherwise. If they become the source of conflict they should be discontinued.

- Rewards should be in response to appropriate behaviour.

- Other class members must not perceive the use of rewards as 'treats for naughty children'.

- Other colleagues must know of and agree to the use of rewards.

- Rewards must fit in to the school's overall behaviour policy.

- Parents must approve of the reward system.

- Rewards must not serve to highlight, expose or label the child. They should be as unobtrusive as possible.

Adjusting the System of Rewards

It is unlikely that any successful teacher will be working without a complex system of rewards and sanctions in use in their classroom. For whatever reason, a child presenting emotional and behavioural difficulties is not responding appropriately to the current system. It is helpful to consider your system against the backdrop of the common features of successful rewards:

1. The pupil knows the specific behaviour expected and the reward they will receive.

2. Reward immediately after or closely following the desired behaviour.

3. Rewards are consistently applied.

4. When the behaviour happens frequently, reinforce patterns of behaviour, e.g. either after it occurs a fixed number of times, or after a set period of time has passed with the desired behaviour evident.

5. If a pupil becomes less interested in the reward, reduce size of or discontinue reward. (If pupils seem unwilling to work for a reward you feel they would like to have, give it once or twice for free and consider increasing the size of the reward.)

6. Avoid the reward becoming routine and mechanical. Have a menu of rewards, e.g. after a few 'well dones', switch to 'you really are working well today'. (Remember the principle of what familiarity can breed.)

7. Always praise. While you may initially be using material rewards and/or activities, praise whenever you give the pupil a reward. (By always giving verbal praise at the same time as your reward, praise will become synonymous with rewards.)

8. Always allow time for any consequences to have an effect.

When you make a decision to adjust the reward system in your classroom, that is when you *formulate* a strategy. Decide on an appropriate time to *implement* the amended system. *Monitor* the results systematically in relation to any child you are concerned about. Finally decide on an appropriate time to *evaluate* its effectiveness.

> Pupils with emotional and behavioural difficulties are more likely to be used to being punished than rewarded by adults.

Choose strategies to change this
- Move the child to another seat away from the source of distractions.

- Focus only on their strengths.

- Use peer support.

- Use stickers, certificates etc.

- Allow time to catch up missed work.

- Use time out, in/outside another class.

- Use hierarchy of positive consequences.

- When necessary give clear verbal cautions in a private setting.

- Reward short periods of appropriate behaviour.

- Negotiate agreed reparations when penalties are needed.

Pupil relationships

> Pupils showing emotional and behavioural difficulties will be more likely to be used to experiencing poor peer relationships.

Choose strategies to change this
- Change peer interactions.

- Set up task-related work partnerships.

- Select groups including your target child to plan class/social activities.

- Develop group/class problem solving activities, e.g. brainstorming.

- Rotate groups for activities.

- Involve focus groups or working parties in finding solutions.

- Increase the range of activities relying on pupils' choice and responsibility.

- Actively deal with bullying. (Your school should have a clear policy on ways to deal with bullying. If the policy is unknown or not working seek to review it. Refer to: Sections 55-57 of DfEE *Circular 8/94* or strategies such as *The No Blame Approach* (1993) or refer to publications such as Besag (1992), Elliot (1991) or Smith and Thompson (1991) for practical suggestions.)

- Use positive role models from films or literature.

Pupil/teacher relationship

Pupils showing emotional and behavioural difficulties are more likely to be used to experiencing negative adult interactions.

Choose strategies to change this
- Be polite, prepared and punctual.

- Use positive non-verbal communication.

- Use active listening skills; check out your understanding.

- Be fair and reasonable.

- Start fresh each day.

- Be hard on issues, caring of people.

- Teach self-control, count to ten and back again.

- Manage by walking around the class.

- Sit with pupils.

- Show them your effort to improve situations.

- Avoid win-lose confrontations.

- Negotiate and compromise.

- Anticipate and prevent problems.

- Involve pupils in decisions.

- Record pupils' efforts and achievements.

- Value them as people.

- Actively listen to the pupils.

Many of these you will be doing at all times or from time to time as circumstances require. When you have registered a concern about a pupil, there is an increased need to be explicit and explain, monitor and evaluate all the strategies you are employing. Remember the cycle of:

FORMULATE, IMPLEMENT, MONITOR, EVALUATE

Always consider the possibility of exiting the cycle after the evaluation stage before returning to formulate a new strategy.

Gathering detailed information helps the teacher to assess progress. Sometimes the best a teacher can hope for is to recognise progress in what can be a slow process with periods of success and periods of remission.

Dealing with emotional and behavioural difficulties may be seen as an intractable and frustrating task for teachers.

(DfEE *Circular 9/94*)

Chapter 4 – Code of Practice Stages 2 and 3

Understanding and Strategies

We have already stressed that most children are naughty at some time. It might even be fairer to say that they are not naughty but just exploring the rules and boundaries around them. This is a normal part of their development. Most children respond very quickly to adult correction. They are generally emotionally secure and well-adjusted – that is, they are happy. The children who are described as disruptive, disaffected, alienated, lack such security. Their difficulties hinder them from readily internalising and accepting either the constraints they meet or the emotional support offered to them.

At *Code of Practice* Stages 2 and 3 your interventions will be more structured and regularly reviewed with all concerned, pupil, teachers, and parents/carers. Some of the strategies will be the same as or extensions of those identified at Stage 1.

Is the pupil unable?	Is the pupil unwilling?
Are they unable to follow instructions?	Do they seem to seek out confrontation with adults?
Is the work appropriate for them?	Do they intimidate and threaten others?
Do they lack social skills?	Do they resent adults making any request of them?
Are they happier playing with younger children?	Do they seem to need to be in control?

Figure 10

Below are a range of strategies aimed at addressing some of the goals you feel the pupil's behaviour is aimed at. Wanting teacher attention is not the problem, it is the way the pupil tries to achieve it. To help you decide the type of strategies to use, ask yourself the following two questions: Is the pupil unable? Or is the pupil unwilling? (See *Figure 10*.)

Of course the child presenting emotional and behavioural difficulties will rarely fit into neat categories. Also the expression of their difficulties may change from time to time. Nonetheless there are useful groupings under which to plan and evaluate strategies. When you have selected your strategy, after carefully reflecting on all of the information you have gained about the child, have the utmost faith that it will work. It is more likely to work if you believe in it. If by some fluke it does not work, the next plan you formulate will be all the better for your increased experience. You will be in a no-lose process.

Information

The following strategies vary considerably in the amount of detail provided. Most are considered to be self-explanatory and so unnecessary detail has been avoided. Others are considered to be too important to be briefly included and so a fuller account has been provided.

> The teacher's task is to choose those methods that best fit their concerns, are appropriate for the pupil and are those that they believe are most likely to be successful.

The problem behaviours that interfere most with a teacher's ability to teach and pupils' ability to learn are those 'acting out' behaviours. These interrupt and disrupt. They also cause negative feelings within the adults who work with them. These feelings can direct the class teacher towards understanding what the pupil may be trying to achieve through their behaviour. Of course, any one behaviour may be serving several different goals. *Figure 11* illustrates the types of feelings engendered by different behaviours and the goals they may be directed towards.

Acting out behaviour	Goal of behaviour	Teacher feelings
off task	attention, task avoidance	frustration, annoyance
destructive	revenge	concern, anger
aggressive	control	fear/anger

Figure 11

Unwilling (Acting Out)
Guidelines
- The behaviour is the problem, not the child.

- Pupils can learn new ways of relating with adults.

- Changes will most likely be resisted by the pupil.

- Use of sensitive humour may help to diffuse situations.

- It is important to maintain self-esteem.

Natural Consequences
A consequence follows on as a result of what a pupil does. If you stay in bed, you will be late for appointments. If you do not put things away, you will be unlikely to find what you want. These are not sanctions, but consequences. A natural or social rule has been broken, so certain consequences follow. Natural consequences are not given with hostility, they are just given. Whereas sanctions so often cause resentment, consequences are more like 'facts of life' and apply to all. When pupils have choices to make, be clear with them what consequences will follow their actions. Natural consequences are what follows when the natural world order is challenged. For example, if you do not eat, you will become hungry. If you leave equipment outside, it will get wet and damaged. Natural consequences that do not threaten the safety of a pupil are acceptable, but children should never be put at risk 'as a learning experience'.

Logical Consequences
Logical consequences would be those that are a violation of the social order, which are rules to enable us to live together. Verbal and physical abuse violates the social order. A pupil who prevents others from working is breaking the social order. Equipment which is not put away correctly will not be ready for next time, which will give less time to complete the set task. Wherever possible pupils should be able to make mistakes and cope with the consequences. These can then be the focus of group or individual discussions at a later date.

Positive Consequence Agreements
Negotiate with the pupil agreed, positive targets and decide penalties and bonuses for all involved. A good agreement means that there is something in it for all parties. Pupils should be willing participants. If it is a one-sided agreement with the pupil having to contribute most and the teacher/adult little, then it is likely to be too one-sided to create a win-win outcome. Parents too can be included in negotiating positive consequences for their children. It is important that the positive consequence is proportionate and does not become a source of stress on the child, e.g. 'If you behave well for a month, I will buy you a mountain bike'. This creates two problems for the pupil. Firstly asking for continuous good behaviour for a whole month for a child with long-standing behaviour difficulties (they must be long-standing if the child is at Stage 2 or 3 of the *Code of Practice*) is probably unrealistic. The prospect of failure is thus heightened. Secondly the high price of the positive consequence is likely to make the donor more demanding. 'I give you all this and look how you treat me in return.' (Refer back to the principles for rewards when establishing a Stage 2 or 3 programme based on the use of positive consequences.)

Time Out

Time out is most effective when it is withdrawal of reinforcement: teacher attention; rewarding activities; friends; points earning; visual or aural stimulation. There will be occasions when a pupil you are teaching behaves in an unacceptable manner. At such times, time out may be helpful. Its aim is to reduce the undesired behaviour that precedes it. It is a consequence of what they have done. It is under their control.

Types of Time Out

• *Isolation time out*

The pupil is removed from the classroom to a time out room for a fixed period. While being well lit and paying regard to the pupil's health and safety, the time out setting should be a boring environment with no displays or distracting objects. Time out rooms need to be set up with a great deal of forethought. They can easily be used as a punishment area, which is not what time out is designed for. The end result of using time out as punishment is that all too often it gets used by the same few pupils and becomes the focus for their anger. It can raise the level of confrontations and encourage graffiti and damage. When managed correctly it can be a very effective control measure.

• *Exclusion time out*

The pupil is removed to the corner of the classroom and excluded from activities.

• *Non-exclusion time out*

The pupil has to sit and watch the appropriate behaviours of other pupils, but is not allowed to join in.

Using time out (guidelines)
• Explain your use of time out to your pupils.

• Use it immediately after undesired behaviour.

• Behave in a matter-of-fact manner.

• Minimise your verbal exchange with the pupil, but explain the behaviour that has led to time out.

• Vary the length of time out with short spells, three to five minutes at a time until an effective period is identified.

• When you first use time out, the pupil may well display aggressive behaviour. Increase the time out for the period of disturbance (seek support, if necessary).

• Reassure the pupil that it is not your wish for them to be in time out, you want them in your lesson. It is their behaviour which has brought about that consequence.

• At the end of time out, return the pupil in a quiet, matter-of-fact manner to regular class activities.

• Return to normality when time out is finished. Do not enter into long discussions, explanations etc.

• Make sure colleagues and the pupil's parents know of your use of this approach.

• Monitor how frequently you use time out and its effect.

Self-Monitoring

This involves two steps, self-observation and self-recording. Firstly the pupil must be able to recognise the behaviour they are to observe. The pupil may record their on/off task behaviour, or how often they leave their seat during an agreed period. Agreed targets can be set with rewards. A pupil who is motivated to change their behaviour will find this method constructive. It is best for pronounced and conspicuous behaviours rather than verbal behaviours. Performance goals, feedback through reviews as well as rewards will all help increase its effectiveness. It is a very good way of obtaining data about certain behaviours. Often pupils are 'amazed' as to how often they do leave their seat for no legitimate reason.

Problem Solving

This involves the pupil working through a number of steps to resolve a difficulty. Problem situations are identified, the feelings involved are described, goal setting, alternative responses, solution selection, rehearsal and implementation are also discussed. The pupil would set acceptable improvement targets as well as having specific rewards.

A basic problem solving model might include the following. The pupil is taught to consider a programme in which they STOP when they recognise a problem situation and REMEMBER the agreed things to do, then ACT. This sequence can be used proactively to help them to face up to predicted future difficulties, e.g. 'When I feel like running out of science I should recognise my feelings and breathe deeply and count backwards from ten. Then I should ask a nominated pupil to help me with the work which I am finding hard.' It can also be used reactively to talk through times when things have gone wrong and discuss what actually happened with what might have happened if the above strategy had been used effectively. (See the Pupil Planning Sheet in Appendix 6.)

Temper Control

There are many reasons why children lack the ability to control emotional outbursts and explode when faced by difficult situations, often during free time with their peers. Discussion around this with the pupils may enable them to recognise the build-up to a loss of temper and to stop... then think of strategies they may use like leaving the room, giving an agreed signal to teacher, deep breathing exercises.

(Strategies to help pupils to recognise their own thinking and feelings come under that area of psychology described as Cognitive Behavioural. There is a growing body of knowledge about the different uses of Cognitive Behavioural Therapies (CBT). This has formed the basis of a whole approach to behavioural difficulties in Australian schools called Stop, Think, Do (ACER). At the time of compiling this book this scheme was unavailable in the UK.)

Attention Seeking Response Plan

The desire for adult attention is a natural feature of children. For most children such attention is obtained through being positive and friendly. Some, however, learn from adults that the only way to obtain attention is through aggressive and demanding behaviour. For them negative adult attention is better than no attention at all. If the pupil is motivated to obtain your attention no matter how – take control of the process. Only give the pupil your attention for appropriate behaviour. Use time out for inappropriate behaviour. Make every effort to catch the pupil behaving well and reinforce positive behaviour. Teach them what to do and what you will pay attention to.

Power Response Plan

Some pupils become very experienced in having confrontations with adults. Teachers can be faced with a seemingly interminable debate or even confrontation. Things can get to a point where the teacher has to accept that if 'good' argument would have sorted matters out, it would have done so by now. The problem would have been solved. A win-lose situation can be overcome by stating your desire to avoid confrontation. Discuss the situation, acknowledge their desire to hold on to control. If possible try to channel this need. Employ logical consequences for behaviour which is disrupting you from teaching and preventing other pupils from learning.

Revenge Response Plan

At times children can feel 'hard done by'. This can lead to feelings of resentment and jealousy. At such times a pupil may seek to either hurt other children or perhaps damage their work. The internal distress seeks to express itself in behaviour in accord with its goal. With such children talk openly about the cause of such strong feelings. Reassure them that the feelings are natural. Help them to understand which behaviours are unacceptable and offer to develop a plan to improve relationships with peers. Set clear boundaries to prevent harm to self and others. At all times care for and support the child while helping them to manage their behaviour. Development of self-esteem will always be appropriate with such children.

Response Cost (Token Economy)

In discussion with the pupil establish a cost for various behaviours – certain desired behaviours carrying a fixed number of points that the pupil can earn. As these mount up the pupil can exchange them for various rewards at different rates. If inappropriate behaviour occurs then the pupil will be 'fined' and the agreed number of penalty points subtracted. The aim should be to ensure that the pupil is earning points and achieving success. Being in the red is not going to motivate anyone. You are trying to teach the pupil that behaviours have consequences and that they are in control of their own behaviour, that is they determine what they get.

Unwilling *Aide-Mémoire*

Unwilling children display defiant aggressive behaviour. Some possible sources of their difficulties are:
- they are finding the work set difficult to manage;

- they have learning difficulties, global or specific, and are experiencing great frustration;

- they are unused to following externally imposed community rules;

- they are used to inconsistent handling and adult capitulation in the face of their tantrums;

- they may be victims of abuse or bullying in or out of school.

The effect on these children can be significant: They may:
- be deeply unhappy;

- be unaware of the consequences of their actions;

- be developing pervasive negative views of their educational experience;

- experience rejection and hostility from peers and adults.

These children are passing on their negative experiences. They need care and support but often spurn it.

Principles

1. The behaviour is the problem not the child.

2. These pupils can learn new ways of relating to others.

3. Behaviour can be strongly related to learning ability.

4. Changes will be resisted by the pupil.

5. Sensitive humour may diffuse some difficult moments with these pupils.

6. Programmes should aim for respect of self, others, property.

Strategies

1. **Consequences:** *Develop logical and natural responses to pupils' behaviour. Negotiate with the pupil a 'possible consequences' agreement.*
2. **Time Out:** *Respond to problem behaviour in a matter-of-fact way which communicates where the boundaries are and crossing them will result in loss of inclusion in your lesson.*
3. **Self-Monitoring:** *The pupil is involved in recording various specific behaviours, e.g. on/off-task; in or out of seat; time spent without interrupting teacher or peers.*
4. **Problem Solving:** *Teach and practice strategies for dealing with difficult situations – Stop ... Think ... Act.*
5. **Temper Control:** *Teach control skills like deep breathing exercises and practice them. Reward periods of time free from temper loss.*
6. **Attention Seeking Response Plan:** *Direct your time and efforts to those pupils presenting appropriate behaviour.*
7. **Power Response Plan:** *Channel the pupil's desire for control and negotiate consequences.*
8. **Revenge Response Plan:** *Provide boundaries that protect the child and others. Talk openly about their behaviour as unacceptable and agree a plan to develop friendships.*
9. **Response Cost:** *Agree a going rate of token rewards for certain desired behaviours.*
10. **Positive Entrapment:** *Spot the pupils being good and reward the spontaneously occurring behaviour.*
11. **Off My Back:** *Increase monitoring etc. Help the pupil to reduce the 'hassle factor'.*

Positive Entrapment

'Acting out' pupils are typically used to receiving negative feedback from adults. To change this we need to surround them with positive feedback. Make a point of noticing them succeeding. Comment on this and ask them to explain to you what it is they have done that you like, and how have they been able to do it. DO NOT ask them why they have done it. The aim is to frequently draw their attention to them behaving appropriately. Have fixed meetings with them to focus on small but positive steps. Set a positive tone to your meetings. Your underlying aim is to show the pupil that they have the solutions already, focus on these and emphasise them.

'Off My Back'

We all know that the most difficult pupils are usually adolescents who do not see any need to change because they have not got a problem. School has a problem, home has a problem but they do not. Pain reduction or in this case 'hassle' can be a motivation. If you arrange frequent checks of a pupil, ask them to report to you frequently, arrange for after-school meetings with home, you are becoming a problem to the pupil. They would probably like to have you 'off their back'. Use this as a lever, motivation. Help them to decide what it is they need to do to reduce your involvement.

Unable

Guidelines

- Social skills can be learned.

- Work in small steps to success.

- Make learning safe and fun.

- Establish what pupil can do.

- Maintain pupil's self-esteem.

Social Interaction Plan

Observe the pupil over a period of time. Carry out a strengths and weaknesses brainstorming of their social skills. This can be done as an individual or group activity. Decide what social skills you would like to see the pupil develop. Acknowledge and reward any you observe the pupil using spontaneously. Keep a record to monitor to see whether these behaviours increase in frequency.

Group Goals

Set a group task e.g. researching and delivering a presentation which can only be achieved through active co-operation with peers. Initially pair the pupil with another who will support and ensure success.

Live Modelling

In discussion with the pupil they are directed to observe instances of a specific social skill which they are to learn and practice. The teacher can act as a sort of commentator on the process of the lesson, pointing out good examples of behaviours which have been identified as those your pupil should be working towards.

Symbolic Modelling

Particular topics can be chosen through PSE lessons. Pupils are then encouraged to watch a video or film, or read appropriate material which gives examples of the skill to be learned. In safe settings they are to practice this skill through role play. This can be approached as a whole class activity but targeted towards helping a pupil or group of pupils to improve on some aspect of their behaviour.

Coaching

Pupil meets with tutor to discuss the need for a certain social skill, for example politeness, or listening skills. Clear rules are given as to how to develop these skills in different circumstances around the school. The pupil then begins to practice these on their own and then with 'friendly' others. Tutor and pupil review progress and set up more practice of the new skill, friendship skills.

Time Programme

Use this when you wish to remove/reduce certain behaviours. A reward is obtained by the pupil when an agreed amount of time has passed without them showing the behaviour, e.g. two weeks with no problems in

Unable *Aide-Mémoire*

There are many reasons why some children experience difficulties in relating to adults and peers. They include:

- illness;

- hearing loss;

- isolated upbringing;

- trauma.

The effect on these children can be significant:

- They may suffer rejection from their peers.

- Their difficulties in mixing may be misconstrued as unwillingness, rudeness or stand-offishness.

These children can be helped to relate better to their peers through sensitive small step programmes.

Principles

1. Social skills can be learnt.

2. Success can be achieved by setting small step targets.

3. It is important first to build on what the child can do. The first step is therefore to identify areas of strength.

4. Children learn best from observing, planning and doing.

5. Learning should be safe and fun.

Strategies

1. **Social Interaction Plan:** *Reward successful interactions, record and monitor.*

2. **Group Goal:** *Child works with group to agreed shared goal.*

3. **Time Programme:** *The pupil is rewarded after fixed periods of time without a specified problem behaviour.*

4. **Peer Support:** *Enlist the active support of peers to help the pupil acquire an increase in desired social behaviour.*

5. **Live Modelling:** *The pupil is directed to observe the specific behaviour in others (through role play perhaps).*

6. **Coaching:** *Describe the desired behaviour, let the pupil practice and then give feedback.*

7. **Cooperative Learning:** *Set learning opportunities which require the pupil to relate positively in pursuit of a shared goal.*

8. **Social Instructional Training:** *To increase self-control in impulsive and aggressive children, the child learns to give themselves instructions to avoid immediate action and to use more effective coping strategies.*

PE = one positive telephone call from teacher to the pupil's parents. Periods of time can be shortened or lengthened depending on success rates.

Self-Instructional Training

There are some children who show impulsive and aggressive behaviour which they feel unable to control. The child may say, 'I don't want to shout at the other children. I don't know what comes over me.' The aim for the child is to teach them to give themselves instructions, to avoid immediate action and to help them cope with minor problems. The training would involve them in repeating to themselves and doing some action which blocked conflict. For example, a boy who would at times explode in anger and knock chairs around when teased was taught to say, 'I will not act now. I will decide in my thinking corner what to do for the best.' This self-control needs lots of practice and appropriate rewards.

Peer Support

Sensitive discussion with other pupils as to how a friend is experiencing difficulties can enable them to actively give support. Positive consequences for their help will increase motivation. Assistance may be as low key as involving the pupil in break time activities. Or it may be through an increased understanding that the pupil has 'difficulties' and requires support to avoid matters worsening. (This can be approached through a well-structured programme with external support from an educational psychologist or a behavioural support teacher. See *Circle of Friends*, Wilson and Newton, 1996.)

Co-operative Learning

A well-used example of this is the 'jigsaw technique'. The class is divided into, say, six to eight groups of four pupils. Each group is going to look at Leisure in the Twentieth Century. In each group one pupil would focus on one of the following: Patterns of work, Health issues, Sport and facilities. Each pupil would have information to research. Each pupil would meet and discuss with members from the other groups who were also working in the same area to exchange information. To complete the assignment each aspect needs to be fully understood and joined with the other parts. The members of each group experience being interdependent and learn the need to co-operate to achieve a satisfactory outcome. For most children this process will be problem free. For the focus child additional support and encouragement can be given either directly or through the pupil group.

Acting In

Many pupils will face barriers to their learning on account of the emotional difficulties and/or stress they face. These will prevent them from learning as they will be less able to concentrate on their work. Emotional difficulties will affect both their behaviour and their ability to think. Remember the distinction we are making between 'acting out' and 'acting in' is one of convenience for us. All children are extremely complicated. An aggressive pupil may be equally anxious and have as little self-confidence as the stereotypical anxious and withdrawn pupil who usually springs to mind. Some of those pupils who are acting out will also be experiencing emotional difficulties and the strategies presented below may be of equal value to them as well.

'Acting in' problem behaviours interfere less with a teacher's ability to teach but interfere certainly with pupils' ability to learn. Like acting out behaviours these too can generate negative feelings within the adults who work with them. These feelings can direct the class teacher towards understanding what the pupil may be trying to achieve through their behaviour. Of course, any one behaviour may be serving several different goals. *Figure12* illustrates the types of feelings engendered by different acting in behaviours and the goals they may be directed towards.

Acting in behaviour	Cause of behaviour	Teacher feelings
over-reliance/attention seeking	low confidence	irritated
passive/withdrawn	depression	helpless
tearful, sensitive	anxiety	sad, concerned

Figure 12

Adolescence

It may be helpful to consider adolescence as a time when pupils are more likely to experience emotional difficulties. This is a period when many changes are taking place. Physically, growth spurts occur and teenagers become prone to being clumsy. Their thought processes are also becoming more adult-like yet they live in a world where many crucial decisions are made for them.

Their powerlessness becomes an issue as their emotional maturity increases. They can now reason in the abstract, and see what is in the world, and what could be. This problem is exacerbated by the adult community around them. Half the time adolescents are told to 'grow up and act their age', and the rest of the time they are told that 'they are getting too big for their boots'. There is also good evidence to suggest that the 'horribleness' of teenagers is a disproportionate and recurrent theme in the press and on TV.

As if all that was not enough, adolescents are increasingly moving towards sexual maturity, and so all of their development is taking place on a shifting bedrock of hormonal changes. There is an ever-present need to reconcile what they have been with what they want to be. It is hardly surprising that with all this going on, the demands and expectations placed on them by adults can cause them to experience difficulties.

In the face of so many demands, their one aspect which is especially vulnerable is their self-esteem. To protect this they often turn to each other and receive support from their peers rather than adults. Just like adults they will rely on internal defence mechanisms. These exist because maintenance of good self-esteem is so important that it cannot be left to chance. *Figure 13* lists the different mechanisms that exist and how they seek to defend the adolescent from low self-esteem through facing painful emotions.

Defence Behaviour	Protection Against	Strategy
withdrawal, emotional withdrawal	isolation/cynicism	real challenging situations
escapism	low self-esteem, fear of failure	avoidance of problem situations
rationalisation	arguments, sour grapes	avoidance of guilt and self-blame
projection	attack of scapegoats or minority groups	avoidance of negative feelings towards self
displacement	negative behaviour towards 'safe' others	prevents danger of confronting real threat

Figure 13

When defence mechanisms are used in moderation they prevent short-term emotional overload and undue stress. But they can be ineffective in the long term as they prevent the individual working towards more positive ways of coping through facing up to the situation.

When Sadness Becomes a Problem

There is a readily understandable link between 'acting out/conduct difficulties' and 'acting in/emotional difficulties'. Both are outward manifestations of inner feelings. The internal emotional unhappiness children experience will be reflected in their behaviour. Also children who are unhappy, stressed, angry etc. will often try, through their behaviours, to create the same feelings in their outside world. So if a child feels anger inside they achieve a sense of consistency and predictability if they can get the adults in their lives to behave aggressively towards themselves. Similarly if a child has a low self-esteem and feels little or no respect for themselves then there will be a psychological need to get people in their world to reject them as they themselves have done.

Children with emotional difficulties are:	• easily hurt • lacking in self-esteem • emotionally volatile

Often children with emotional difficulties/disorders have lost trust in adults. They will often be highly resistant to attempts made by adults to get close to them. We must try to support them in acknowledging their feelings. Remember being angry is not a problem. Anger is a normal and often appropriate feeling. The difficulty is the flight or fight behaviour it can give rise to. Such children will need to help understand their feelings and ways of coping with them.

A way in which we can help explain the behavioural difficulties children experience through their emotional needs is presented below with intervention suggestions which may be adapted to your particular circumstances. It is again worth stressing that supporting children with EBD is more like an art than it is a science. It is difficult to generate direct cause and effect relationships. It is the teacher's knowledge and understanding of a child which will inform them as to how to best offer support.

Evidence does suggest that many children who experience life stressors such as family bereavement, serious illness, family discord, new family members, experience more problems in school in such areas as peer relationships, frustration tolerance and rule following (Alsop and McCaffrey, 1993). We must emphasise here that it is neither possible nor right for a teacher to take on the responsibility of helping their pupils cope with all the stressful events they may experience, but they can make a difference. The teacher's attitude and understanding can have a real positive effect in supporting and reducing a child's distress.

To help you decide the type of strategies to use, ask yourself the following two questions:

Is the pupil unhappy?
Indicators:

- low personal confidence;

- avoidance of activities they once enjoyed;

- avoidance of eye contact and unusual passivity;

- lack of a sense of purpose and control in their life.

Is the pupil over-anxious?
Indicators:

- over-sensitivity to criticism;

- setting unrealistic targets for themselves;

- imagining the worst in any given situation (generally pessimistic);

- inability to relax.

Unhappy: guidelines
- Unhappy children will be emotionally volatile;

- what they most avoid is often what they most desire;

- they will need time and patience to trust adults;

- they will be trying to create in the outside world the feelings they have inside;

- unhappy children lack the confidence to take on new challenges.

Strategies
Unconditional positive regard
Children will often seek to engender in the adults around them the negative feeling they hold about themselves. One way of monitoring your own feelings in any work with a child is to seek always to have a positive regard for them. Even in the face of difficulties, make time to be with the pupil. Show them that you enjoy spending time with them, that they are important and valued in their own right. Most importantly show a willingness to start with 'a clean slate'.

Empathic support

Listen to their difficulties and consider what are the feelings that cause them pain. Show care and understanding of their situation. Do not deny the pain they are going through. Empathetic statements, like 'I wish I could make it different,' are a way of accepting their pain and showing your desire to help them.

Inadequacy response programme

Carefully plan successes for the pupil. Build on existing strengths. Involve the pupil in setting small achievable targets. Check that they have the ability to meet the demands of the tasks.

Status tasks

Involve the pupil in tasks that carry status in the class or school. Give them manageable tasks which involve increased responsibility. If they are not ready to take on responsibility, could they support another pupil in some area of responsibility (e.g. setting up the OHP for morning hymn practice, or tidying away the gym equipment)? Involve the pupil in recording their successes and send progress notes home.

Anger Management

Anger is a normal and healthy response to many situations, such as family discord, bereavement, friendship disputes, difficult work. Other causes of anger in young people can come from the pressures that home, school and society put on them to 'grow up'. Skills which can help those involved deal with the anger are:

* *disengaging* – the pupil selects a set of activities to go and do when they sense that they are likely to become aggressive; a special corner with pre-chosen activities;

* *displacement activities* – to release the anger the pupil may be directed towards some physical activity, such as tearing up polystyrene to make a bean bag (such activities need to be carefully managed because they can quickly become the source of difficulties through the pupil themselves or other class members interfering);

* *elective time out* – a place where a pupil can opt to go, to calm down before rejoining the class. A pupil would practice using this and be praised for its successful use, but not at the time when they are using it. (The acceptable limits of this approach need to be agreed with the pupil beforehand. They may resort to the use of such a strategy incrementally. It is vital, therefore, that elective time out is systematically monitored.)

Self-esteem development

Self-esteem comprises three main components.

* *Value:* the feelings a pupil has about their place in the community, their friendship group, their relationship with their teacher/tutor etc.

* *Control:* the pupil's ability to master the demands placed upon them by themselves through perfectionism, or by others through peer group pressure or through the school academic demands.

* *Competency:* the pupil's estimate of their abilities. These will be reliant on the processes for the identification and acknowledgment of the pupils' skills and talent.

To enhance self-esteem, programmes should be designed to address the three areas above together, e.g.:

* Make special time available to the pupil (value).

* Design 'I can ...' record card that pupil is expected to fill in at least three out of five each day (competency).

* Utilise their strengths – could they help another pupil (control)?

* Discuss and involve pupil in plan (value).

* Record effort (control) and achievements (competence).

* Find good news to celebrate each day (value).

(See Appendix 6 The Pupil Planner for a framework to use in this approach.)

Unhappy *Aide-Mémoire*

Unhappy children often present no serious management difficulty in the classroom. They are of concern because they:

- are underachieving;

- may be at greater risk of being bullied;

- may be experiencing unbearable home circumstances.

The effect on these children can be significant: They may:
- suffer low self-esteem;

- have a lack of a sense of personal value;

- be developing pervasive views of their educational experience;

- gain poor experience on which to base their future learning.

These children can be helped to develop a greater sense of personal worth.

Principles

1. Unhappy children will be emotionally volatile.

2. They avoid most what they most want.

3. They are trying to create in the outside world the feelings they have inside.

4. They need to build up trust which takes time and patience.

5. They will lack confidence to take on new challenges.

Strategies

1. **Unconditional Positive Regard:** *Put aside special time to be with the child to show you value them.*
2. **Anger Management:** *Teach children that feelings are OK. It is aggressive behaviour that needs controlling. Teach them skills to manage their inner feelings.*
3. **Positive Thinking:** *Teach statements which recognise their strengths.*
4. **Empathetic Support:** *Acknowledge the pain children experience: 'That must make you feel really bad' or 'I wish I could make things better for you.'*
5. **Inadequacy Response Programme:** *Carefully plan a programme of successes for the pupil, e.g. return to work they have enjoyed and successfully completed.*
6. **Status Tasks:** *Involve the pupil in tasks that carry status in the class or school, perhaps supporting another pupil who is familiar with the task.*
7. **Self-Esteem Development:** *Plan each day to develop their control and competence and discuss improvements to show that you value them.*
8. **Control Programme:** *Increase the pupil's locus of control. The pupil is to set targets and monitor progress against them.*
9. **Act As If:** *Use role play to let a child practice behaving in ways they would like to, e.g. dealing with bullying. Find safe ways to develop assertive behaviour.*
10. **Random Acts of Kindness:** *Plan and celebrate certain daily 'good deeds'.*
11. **Self-Care:** *Teach the pupil to think and act positively about themselves each day.*

Control Programme

Related to self-esteem, this will involve setting the pupil targets which they will decide and how they are to achieve them. The aim is to increase 'locus of control'. This is a person's belief in being in charge and able to control or effect events in their life. People who believe they are externally controlled tend to have lower self-esteem and do not feel they can change whatever is happening to them. Your goal would be to help the pupil realise what they had achieved through their own efforts. The steps with passive or depressed pupils would naturally be extremely small but that does not matter. The experience of achieving a set goal through their own effort is what matters.

Positive Thinking

Produce a list of statements about what the pupil has achieved, their qualities etc. They will be expected to learn these off by heart and practice them at set times of the day. They may also have certain words which they are to repeat at times of challenge, for example 'will', 'can', 'control' etc.

Act As If

At times when pupils lack confidence or feel sad and depressed this is a simple technique which can help. Pupils need to practice how to stand, look and behave etc. for certain emotions. Then even when they lack the feeling they wish to have, they are able to 'act as if' they had it. If pupils walk around with drooped shoulders and eyes cast downward, then their negative mood will be reinforced. This method tries to break that.

Random Acts of Kindness

When children do something positive and perhaps help others this lifts their spirits and makes them feel better about themselves. Any act such as caring for animals or doing a meaningful task for an adult will help. If they are able to support other children in some area or if perhaps they have either knowledge or a skill, this will be extremely beneficial.

Self-Care

An activities programme is worked out for them to do each day. This would involve some form of appropriate physical exercise, relaxation tasks, positive thinking, recreational activities. The pupil is encouraged to discuss progress against this chart at fixed intervals. Caring for one aspect of their development can naturally or through teacher reference be linked to caring for other areas. It is a sort of Weight Watchers approach to developing personal awareness.

Anxious

Guidelines

- Anxious children have learnt a way of avoiding challenges;

- they will often have generated fears about what 'may' happen;

- they may have a fear of failure which prevents them trying;

- they will be extremely scared of their intense feelings of anxiety;

- they may have learnt that adults are not able to understand or help them.

Relaxation programme

There are almost as many ways of relaxing as there are people. It is important that pupils explore to find the way that helps them. Necessary to all, though, will be the need to relax the muscles and to breathe slowly.

Muscle relaxation

This is simple, quick, any time, any place.
1. Focus on different muscles. Start with your feet and systematically work upwards throughout the body.

2. Tense the muscles; try to hold them tense for six to ten seconds.

3. Then relax, feel the tension disappear.

4. Do this with your feet, legs, arms etc.

5. Pay attention to calm, deep, rhythmical breathing.

6. This will relax you.

Breathing

Breathe in deeply, slowly through your nose, trying to count slowly to four as you do. Now as you breathe out through your mouth, keep pushing the air out for as long as you can. Now practice, breathe in 1, 2, 3, 4, and out. Think as you breathe out how all the tension is going as well.

Thought Control

Adolescents will be prone to having certain negative thoughts which dominate their thinking. The pupil is encouraged to accept that these thoughts are 'irrational' or 'silly'. When this point is reached through discussion or counselling it can be reinforced through the pupil 'dressing' them up, by associating them with certain colours, dress, sounds or music. So that whenever they begin to think them, all these other cues remind them that they are 'silly and irrational'. If this proves hard, they may wear an elastic band on their wrist which they 'ping' whenever certain thoughts come along, to remind them that these are irrational thoughts.

Problem Solving Ladder

If a pupil is anxious about a specific situation then try to break it down into small rungs on the ladder. This can be done visually through drawing the ladder on a paper and writing on each rung a step towards resolution. The steps must be small enough for the pupil to be able to work on with some success. If there is no progress, introduce 'more rungs'. By giving the pupil success in small steps you are also teaching them that they can have some control over their anxiety. This method will probably need to be used in conjunction with some form of relaxation.

Panic Control

Panic is what happens when both anxiety and fear combine. The result is an intense feeling of fear and terror. Panic is a normal reaction to potentially life-threatening situations, but panic attacks do occur in ordinary situations. When this happens panic is not a helpful response. Panic can be understood, managed and unlearnt.

Panic needs
- Negative thoughts;

- fast and shallow breathing;

- a desire to run away.

The process of a panic attack is frightening in itself. The pupil gets into a cycle where they become frightened of fear. The pupil needs to accept what they are feeling, recognise the build-up to a panic attack, and understand that panic is a feeling which cannot harm them. They can:

- learn to relax muscles;

- breathe deeply and slowly;

- stay where they are;

- focus on what they want to do and do it;

- focus on positive thinking;

- talk sense to themselves (I can handle this, I will be OK etc.).

Help a pupil appreciate that we all spend a lot of time worrying about things that never happen. We need to strengthen our positive thoughts which tend to get ignored. As we have some control over our thoughts, pupils can be given several positive thoughts about themselves to learn.

1. One thing I like about myself is ...

2. I'm at my best when I …

3. My favourite holiday was …

4. I know I can …

Pupils can make up their own and learn them off by heart, just like spellings. They then have set times during the day when they rehearse them. Why let the negative thoughts have it all their own way?

Creative Materials

Often the worries and behavioural difficulties that children experience are quite 'normal'. It can help to give children books with stories that reflect similar difficulties to what they are going through. It can also be a helpful way of talking to the child about their worries, one removed from themselves. *Joby* by Stan Barstow is an excellent account of a young man facing up to a variety of potential stressors.

Stability Zones

We each tend to have certain rituals and routines that happen throughout the day for us to unwind. We rarely go from one intensive activity to another, even if we only look out of the window and daydream or have a coffee. For an anxious pupil it is worth setting up a programme of such activities throughout their day and evening to help them relax.

Anxiety Management Through Positive Thinking

What is it that causes anxiety? Develop a plan of action to deal with the situation. What will they say and do? Practice regularly:

I can cope with this.
I know what I am going to do.
Things will get better if I …
I can relax.
I know what anxiety is.
I will be able to cope.

Review

Help the pupil to look at how things went, at what helped and what did not. What could they do next time to make things better? Use the outcome of these meetings to develop positive thinking strategies. Encourage the pupils to reflect on issues they have raised in review meetings when they have reported coping well with a situation. Exploring past areas of success can be much more effective than in-depth exploration of a recent failure, e.g. 'Remember a few weeks ago when you managed to cope with Mr … telling you off. What was special about that time that helped you cope better? What could you learn from that for future situations like this?'

I can cope with anxiety by …
I know if something like this happens again I will try to …
I know that I have made progress despite this setback and I will keep on doing so …

Perfectionist Management

Pupils who strive for perfection are often prone to anxiety. Their desire for perfection can inhibit their everyday functioning as assignments come to dominate them. Discuss your concerns with pupils.

• Develop relaxation techniques.

• Challenge 'I must', 'I should' statements.

• Encourage the pupil to change how they think: 'It would be better if … but if I don't – I am still an OK person.'

• Set clearly defined goals for set periods of time.

• Set targets that are appropriate for the pupil to experience not having completely finished.

• Discuss how they feel and cope with this.

- Develop a programme for the pupil to monitor and decrease their need for perfectionism.

- Build in rewards for the pupil for 'accomplishing their task of not having to accomplish'.

Peer Support

A 'buddy' system can usefully involve a pupil in other activities. Pupils are usually fully aware of their peers who face difficulties. Depending on the nature of the difficulty it may be possible for friends to actively support. For example, if the concern is lack of friends, isolation, withdrawal, then a buddy system may be ideal.

Anxious *Aide-Mémoire*

A certain level of anxiety is normal and helpful. Too much can be extremely frightening. Children may experience excessive anxiety for many reasons. Some examples are:
- through early childhood experiences they may have developed irrational thinking styles;

- ongoing poor adult-child relationships (at the extreme end possible abuse);

- they may have experienced significant trauma;

- they may have an anxious disposition which is reinforced by parenting.

The effect on these children can be significant: They may:

- experience panic attacks (the child may become frightened of fear);

- be construed as uncooperative or rude by adults and peers.

These children are often trapped into patterns of behaviour which their anxiety constrains them from changing,

Principles

1. Anxious children avoid new situations.

2. Anxious children worry about what 'may' happen.

3. They fear failure.

4. They are scared by the intensity of their feelings of fear.

5. Coping skills can be learnt.

Strategies

1. **Relaxation Programme:** *Find a method of relaxing which suits the pupil and teach them to relax on a daily basis. Emphasise the need for breathing control.*

2. **Thought Control:** *Teach the pupil to recognise certain irrational thoughts and discuss ways to reduce their impact.*

3. **Problem Solving Ladder:** *Identify specific focus of anxiety and develop coping skills in small achievable steps.*

4. **Panic Control:** *Teach the pupil to understand panic and explore ways to cope and manage it.*

5. **Creative Materials:** *Use books, films, theatre, art to view the difficulty 'one remove' from themselves. This can enable more safe learning.*

6. **Stability Zones:** *Plan days to include relaxation activities to help the pupil unwind.*

7. **Positive Thinking:** *Teach the pupil 'I can cope' statements to repeat to themselves when faced with difficulties.*

8. **Perfectionist Management:** *Involve the pupil in a range of tactics which enable them to set and reach realistic goals.*

9. **Peer Support:** *Sensitive involvement of key friends can help a child to feel that they are not isolated through their anxiety.*

Bereavement

There are times when it is very normal for a child to feel anxious or unhappy. Bereavement is one such life event which produces very different reactions in individuals. Some become totally reliant on the support of those around them, others will shun the help you may offer.

> Give sorrow words: the grief that does not speak
> Whispers the o'er-fraught heart, and bids it break.
> Shakespeare

Over recent years we have become more sensitive to and understanding of the losses that children experience and how such can affect them. Losses can range from those of pets, to changes in teachers, or from friends moving away to the death of a parent. Depression is quite naturally a part of bereavement, which is in itself a 'healing process'. There will be some pupils whose reaction to their loss is not a source of undue concern. It is such that a class teacher/SENCO will feel they are providing the most appropriate support under the circumstances.

When children experience a loss their reactions are similar to those adults would experience. Thankfully children seem to have a 'shorter span of sadness', and will therefore experience pain for shorter periods of time. While the very young do not understand death, they clearly have grief reactions. The fact that babies will cry when their care-giver leaves a room shows this to be so.

Understanding loss

When we experience the loss of a loved one our world is shattered. This, for children, is like having your protector and provider taken away. A child may now feel that they are in danger and their reaction is to protest. We may talk about their crying being a screaming, calling cry. When their loved one does not return they enter a phase of mourning. This shows that they have accepted the loss of their loved one and are now grieving for them. The crying that may now occur is more of a deep sobbing, a letting go. The final phase is readjusting to life without the loved one.

While we should support children through this period, we must accept that they need to grieve, and that tears are normal. Often children may feel it wrong to cry, and adults may feel an urge to 'change the subject', to 'cheer them up'. If we think of what happens to us when we cut ourselves we can perhaps understand that mourning is a natural process. First we bleed, then the blood clots, a scab is formed before finally a scar is left. We cannot expect to love people and not to be pained when they leave us or die.

Children may talk about 'feeling helpless' or of 'going to pieces'. They may feel for a time that they no longer fit the world. We need to fall apart to come back together and cope without our loved one. We never get over such a loss but we do learn to cope better.

During such times a child will be in 'a dark tunnel'. They may well not hear the support that is offered. They are not yet ready to heal. If we can appreciate what they are going through, we will continue to offer the support because it is the right thing to do. When they are ready, a chink will appear in the tunnel, and they will notice the support that they are being offered. This shows that they are ready to move on.

Figure 14 shows the main phases that children go through and the possible effects on how children think, feel and behave. It also shows the tasks for each stage. It helps only to understand the process; any individual child will be where they need to be and their reactions will be specific to them. The healing process is a journey of grief. Some may pass through it quite quickly. For others it takes a lot longer. They can get stuck, or need to go back.

Model of Loss

Phases of Mourning	Protest	Despair	Adjust
emotions	numbness, shock, anger	sadness, confusion, acute denial	reorganisation, coming to terms, longing
behaviours	argumentative and disobedient	tearfullness, loss of appetite and sleep	new friends and activities
thoughts	questioning why?	I can't cope	I have sad memories but I can cope
tasks of mourning	accept the reality of loss	experience grief	detach and adjust to life without the loved one

Figure 14

Bereavement key issues

- Children's understanding of death will vary with age.

- To avoid pain children may deny the loss and even show the opposite emotion.

- They may displace feelings of pain on to another less important event, e.g. death of a pet. This can allow the pain for the loved one to be released in a manageable way.

- Children may develop obsessional thoughts to do with death.

- They may have aggressive outbursts that release emotions and produce attention, and become withdrawn and isolated.

- Children may display a lack of interest in life and have a poor self-image.

- They may develop physical symptoms such as anxiety at going to school. Headaches and loss of appetite may occur.

> Despite your understanding of the likelihood of psychosomatic reactions, whenever a child complains of physical illness it is always advisable to consult a medical practitioner: the school doctor or the pupil's GP.

Common effects of parental loss

- Night fears;

- sadness;

- anger;

- depression;

- crying;

- irritability;

- regression;

- behaviour changes;

- anxiety;

- increased delinquency;

- increased illness;

- separation difficulties;

- poor school work;

- management problems;

- withdrawal;

- dependent/clinging;

- seek substitute.

Any of the above may change in the pupil's behaviour and can be a result of the loss. Their reactions are not dissimilar to those of adults. The process, timing and pattern of responses differ through the developmental influences.

Consider referring on to the Child and Adolescent Mental Health Services through the educational psychologist or the school's Medical Officer or through the child's own GP. Discuss your concerns if:

- a bereaved child is clearly pretending nothing has happened;

- a child denies that they have lost anyone;

- the child talks or threatens self-harm or suicide;

- they become persistently aggressive;

- they become socially withdrawn and isolated;

- they become involved with anti-social acts such as substance abuse or stealing;

- suicide was the cause of death, which can be especially difficult for a child.

How can class teachers/form tutors help?
When a child suffers a loss they battle to regain the past, to turn the clock back. Anyone who seems to stand in their way is likely to face their anger. We need to show them we understand, but not collude through denying the reality that has happened. 'I understand that you are angry with the doctors because they could not save mum even though they tried so hard.' We need to combine sympathy and understanding while trying to help them accept reality.

Awareness of the 'task of mourning' (see *Figure 14*) will shed light on how a child is responding and will give you some idea as to which they are working on. We need to look sensitively at the stories they are telling us.

As children express their grief, they gain mastery over the loss they have suffered. Be open with children, find out their fears before reassuring them. Children will normally work through their grief at their own pace. Often we need only to be with them. It is unwise and unnecessary to exert pressure on a child to respond in accord with what we 'think they should be doing'.

Principles
- Be open and honest.

- Talk about good and difficult family memories.

- Accept a child's feelings.

- Be a good listener when needed.

- Accept all questions; be honest when the answer is 'I don't know'.

- Show empathy, 'I wish it was different'.

- Offer time, brief but regular.

- Be aware of special days, tickets to school concerts etc.

Most bereaved children are better by the end of the first year.

Strategies
Always make contact with the parent/carer. Remember that in the case of the death of one parent the other will be grieving as well as the child. Listen to their concerns and discuss ways of supporting. Maintain contact and do not take any unilateral action. You may be repeating something others have done with the child but worse still you may make carers feel guilty for not having thought of your suggestion themselves. The formal strategies discussed in each of the sections above will be appropriate for the bereaved child. Below is a list of things to consider when deciding on a strategy to use:

- Ask the child how they would like to be supported.

- Provide bolt holes (agreed ways of withdrawing from groups when in distress).

- Form a support circle.

- Contact CRUSE Bereavement Care (the voluntary counselling service for the bereaved).

- Give permission to grieve.

- Give them time and attention.

- Maintain self-esteem inputs.

- Establish routines.

- Involve child's special friends.

- Offer concentration strategies.

- Create a special 'memory album'.

- Visit church with the pupil.

- Allow the pupil to make a memorial.

- Arrange final 'goodbyes'.

Depression

While all children experience feelings of sadness, it is now recognised that some children, and especially some teenagers, are prone to depression. Between 7 and 14 per cent of children suffer depression before they are 15 years old. As the *Code of Practice* is intended to apply to those barriers that children face to their learning, it is appropriate to include depression. Depression is also becoming more prevalent. The account below, while brief, will include some consideration of suicide – the most extreme and tragic result of depression.

> Depression describes a much more negative emotion than 'sad' or 'fed up'. It is like a fog descending in the mind, which drains effort and prevents decisions being made.

Like most complicated moods, there are likely to be many factors involved. Hormonal changes play an important role – this helps explain why it is more common during the teenage years. Real events can lead to depression. If a young person experiences a series of 'sad' events then vulnerability increases. Such events could include:

- unexpected poor exam results;

- argument with a friend;

- loss of a favourite object;

- a favourite relative moves away.

Each of these events on their own would probably not result in depression. But when they add up by coming in close succession, they can cause strong feelings of despair, helplessness and a lack of control. (As indicated earlier, control is one of the core components of self-esteem.) In such circumstance when a final significant event occurs the child feels trapped in the 'pit' of depression. Once in this pit there is a tendency for the depression to take on a force of its own; that is, it seeks out more negative news to maintain itself. In other words when we become depressed and fall into the pit, instead of climbing out, we carry on digging.

Teachers are clearly concerned with those pupils who are beginning to show signs of depression, with a resultant fall in their work. Pupils who are seriously depressed (see signs of serious depression, below) will need to be referred on quickly. Many researchers believe that mood disorders – such as depression in children and teenagers represent one of the most under-diagnosed illnesses.

Signs of depression

Children experience essentially the same moods as adults but will have different symptoms. Children will often not have the vocabulary to explain what they are feeling and may therefore express their problems through their behaviour. Some of the behaviours associated with depression include:

- sad expressions;

- prone to illnesses;

- poor appetite or overeating;

- poor concentration;

- difficulty in making decisions;

- feelings of hopelessness;

- lack of interest in usual activities;

- little spontaneity/enthusiasm;

- irritability;

- emotionally volatile, tearful;

- frequent negative self-statements;

- hatred of self and everything around them;

- disruptive behaviour;

- unexpected onset of poor learning;

- self-destructive;

- poor peer relationships;

- mood change not a reaction to bereavement or similar loss.

Depression can be associated with substance abuse.

Guidelines

- Be aware of pupils who are passive and withdrawn and reassure them that there is hope, matters can improve.

- Avoid phrases such as, 'come along' and 'cheer up', or 'It can't be that bad'.

- Reassure them that you will stay with them.

- Be persistent in expressing your concerns about them.

- Be sensitive and guided by their response to physical contact. Be sensitive to the feelings they cause in you.

- Aim to offer definite practical help.

Depression, like all human moods, is complicated. We each know sadness and can feel that we know what depression is about. But the pain of depression can be far worse than a physical pain. This internal pain of worthlessness and hopelessness pervades. The individual comes to think poorly of themselves and can then act in ways that get others to respond to them in a similar manner. As they experience rejections from people they know, the pupil feels worse and becomes more and more isolated.

At such times it is not uncommon for depressed teenagers to engage in anti-social behaviour, and to become extremely hostile to people close to them. The internal logic in this is that they are creating in the minds of others the same negative attitudes and feelings they themselves are experiencing. Their depression will try to prevent them asking for help; instead the only solution to ending the pain is suicide.

Confidentiality vs. need to know

This is clearly an issue of importance when we are working with children who need to feel they can trust the adult they are talking with. In counselling the issue of confidentiality is of central importance and much has been written about it. In our context, however, we are working as teachers. We will be employing skills used in counselling, but that does not make us counsellors. Neither should we feel any qualms about using them. Confidentiality refers to the professional responsibility of counsellors.

A pupil may give us information that suggests that they are in real danger. At such times it is our responsibility to inform other relevant agencies. While we may feel that we are betraying a confidence, the young person's safety must be paramount. Depression is a potentially life-threatening disorder. It is hard for us to appreciate that a child is trying to contain intense feelings of anger, rage, hatred and violence. The final act of suicide is an expression of such feelings.

Signs of serious depression
- Marked change in personality;

- dramatic and sudden decrease in school work;

- verbal threats of suicide;

- involvement in anti-social/delinquent behaviour;

- no interest in appearance;

- social isolation;

- emotionally volatile;

- discarding of prized possessions;

- preoccupation with death;

- possession of dangerous weapons e.g. knives;

- sudden cheerfulness after prolonged depression.

Pupils at possible risk of suicide
- Pupils who have already attempted suicide;

- pupils whose parent or close relative committed suicide (there is a risk of post-traumatic stress disorder);

- children with attention deficit disorder will have experienced poor social relationships with peers and can experience feelings of isolation, rejection and feelings of inadequacy. During adolescence this can coincide with them becoming self-centred and comparing themselves with others;

- pupils involved with alcohol and/or substance abuse;

- adolescents struggling with issues of sexuality. Research indicates that gay and lesbian teenagers attempt suicide at a rate of two to three times higher than their heterosexual peers;

- when a media figure dies or commits suicide it is not uncommon for vulnerable adolescents to copy.

Referring on

The *Code of Practice* is intended to be a framework to help teachers meet the needs of pupils with difficulties. After home, teachers spend the most time with pupils and get to know them extremely well under a host of different circumstances. With most children who become depressed they will respond to positive care and support at the early stages. If you have concerns as to whether your approach is suitable or whether the child requires more specialist help, refer on. Depression is a real risk factor for suicidal behaviour. Each week two or three teenagers commit suicide and many thousands receive treatment over the year because of self-inflicted injury.

If in doubt, refer on.

Strategies

Daily action plan

Design with the pupil a programme for them to follow each day. The process of drawing up the plan in itself offers reassurance to the pupil that you are 'with them' through the difficult time. The plan should include where to go, what to do during free times etc. Having a clear schedule can help to reduce feelings of anxiety or possible damaging spells alone at break times. Build in contingencies for times if the pupil is feeling grossly unhappy. Alert colleagues to this plan so that they will be aware of where the pupil should be and what they should be doing.

Control activities

Self-esteem involves control. Encourage the pupil to decide on a range of goals. Point out the areas of choice they have within their current life. Support and help them in making decisions about their work interests etc. Guide them towards setting realistic priorities in their life and an acceptance of their current limitations. (As the song says: 'If you can't be with the one you love, love the one you're with.')

Problem free talk

As part of your work with the pupil spend time discussing their interests, experiences etc. What skills and qualities does this tell you about them? Can you use these skills to raise their confidence, increase their sense of value and purpose? When they feel exceptionally low and talk about their helplessness you can relate back to some of the things they have told you during 'problem free talk' to illustrate areas of strength or times when they have coped.

Short-term target setting

Set small targets each day and review progress. Reaching a target raises self-esteem, while missing a target has the opposite effect. By setting daily targets the prospect of achievement is raised. Unsuccessful experiences can be redressed quickly and setbacks learnt from. Your daily involvement can also be a useful scaffold from which the pupils will start to build their own self-confidence. Watch carefully for the signs the pupil will give you when they are ready to 'go it alone for longer spells'.

'When' and 'will' (not 'if' and 'might')

Make sure that your conversations and planning sessions orient around the solution not the problem. Practice discussing with the pupil what has happened that shows areas of increasing confidence, what they will do when they are in a positive frame of mind, then set about doing this - in small steps, looking for the improvements that will happen.

No more 'ought' and 'should'

Gently challenge negative thinking. Do they think they should be top in a subject? Do they feel they should be liked by everyone? Try to agree on personal expectations which are in the realms of the possible. Through close liaison check that their families' expectations are realistic.

A confidant

Depression can be in part caused by the child experiencing rejection from adults. If there is a preferred teacher, support them in making time to take an interest in the pupil's welfare.

A brilliant corner

Find an area of interest or skill that the pupil has and promote it. Encourage them to make a presentation, write a booklet, produce a piece of artwork, or talk to a reporter from the school magazine. Let them teach

Depression *Aide-Mémoire*

Depression is more than 'everyday sadness' which is a natural emotion. Depression is typified by overwhelming sadness. It is often associated with:

- substance abuse;

- eating disorders;

- the experience of significant trauma;

- a disposition towards negative feelings which is reinforced by life experiences.

The effect on these children can be significant. They are likely to:

- show a significant change in their behaviour;

- show reduced activity levels;

- develop pervasive feelings of helplessness and worthlessness;

- become preoccupied with their inside world;

- become socially isolated.

Depression can appear quickly or over a long period of time. It is not something that the pupil can snap themselves out of.

Principles

1. Depression affects the whole child's behaviour, attitude, etc.

2. It can be reinforced by a series of everyday negative events.

3. It becomes more common in adolescence.

4. Depression can result in self-harm or become life-threatening.

5. It is a serious difficulty, possibly requiring medication, about which the class teacher should seek advice and support … If in doubt refer on.

Strategies

1. **Daily Action Plan:** *Plan each day with the pupil so they know where they can go at critical times especially in free times.*
2. **Problem Free Talk:** *Spend time with the pupil discussing their interests. Note the skills and qualities they have in order to feed back to them at appropriate times.*
3. **Confidant:** *Sensitive involvement of key friends can help a child feel that they are not being rejected. Establish a regular link with a preferred adult.*
4. **Positive Thinking:** *Teach the pupil several positive statements to repeat to themselves when faced with difficulties. Focus on 'when' and 'will'.*
5. **A Brilliant Corner:** *Find a particular skill the pupil has or could develop and allow them to make a classroom display.*
6. **Social Skills Assessment:** *Check that the pupil has the necessary social skills within the class group. If not, teach them through social skills exercises in PSE.*
7. **Pupil Home/School Plan:** *Meet together with family to establish relationships and support for any plans.*
8. **A Daily Happy Programme:** *Develop activities aimed at raising the self-esteem of the pupil.*

other pupils if appropriate. (Protect them from the rigours that class teachers are paid to endure.) You might try doing a joint lesson on their subject. Be careful though, as the other pupils might want a go at this too ...

Social skill assessment

So often a pupil's depression is caused by poor peer relationships on account of their under-learned social skills. If this is the case then a programme to help them learn such skills will be needed. (See section on Unable Pupils.)

Pupil, home and school plan

The source of the pupil's difficulty will often be outside the school. In such cases the teacher can be a useful go-between, e.g. a parent might report to you that they have terrible difficulties with their child at bedtimes. The child's protests turn into confrontations. Discuss their concerns. Set up a plan with the parents and pupil for them to carry out and for you to monitor their progress positively. The end result could be to improve classroom performance.

A daily happy programme

A good way to improve a pupil's self-esteem, is to support them in:

- taking up a social activity that involves exercise and music;

- each day helping them focus on the positive through sharing 'good news';

- ensuring appropriate differentiation for their academic self-esteem;

- if you cannot combine all three, any one or two will be beneficial.

The pain that children/teenagers experience comes in waves and then recedes. They may remain in pain but this is less severe. Therefore they can be seen and talked with only hours before they attempt suicide. There can even be an improvement in their mood as if the making of this final decision has lifted a great burden from them.

Individual Education Plans Guidelines

At Stage 2 the class teacher will have already considered and employed a range of low-level interventions. Having considered a large number of ways in which children with emotional and behavioural difficulties can be supported we may try to use too many. Try to be clear about your aims, long and short term, and your specific objectives. Then choose those strategies you feel will enable you to ensure success.

Remember that it is important not only for the pupil to succeed but for the teachers and other adults involved to feel that their efforts are being rewarded also. While you may already have your own record form for IEPs the one presented below is aimed at you being able to use this book as effectively as possible (see *Figures 15* and *16.*)

Always begin with some understanding of the pupil in mind.

- Who needs to be involved at the planning stage?

- Who needs to be involved in implementation?

The most effective IEPs will have the active participation, support and ownership of the senior management team in the school. Indeed, where this is not embodied in the process the IEP will almost certainly fail to produce results.

- What are the pupil's strengths?

- What internal resources do they have?

- How can you involve them in moving forward?

Remember to focus on behaviour.

Step one: the concern

- What is the concern? Describe it in clear objective terms.

- Where does it happen?

- What time of day?

- Who else is involved?

- How is it affecting the pupil's learning?

- What key information has already been obtained? (See question sheet on page 28.)

NAME OF CHILD: Paul Linforth	DOB: 1.2.86	Class/yr group: 5 LG
DATE OF ACTION: 10.1.96	REVIEW DATE: 6.4.96	
SUPPORT SERVICES INVOLVED: Advice from EP at consultation meeting		

NATURE OF CONCERN
High incidence of off-task behaviour 75%+ as measured in three observations in first week of term. Very argumentative with teacher when told off. Disputes with other pupils. Some temper tantrums. This is the second of two Stage 2 programmes.

TARGETS	MONITORING	CRITERIA FOR SUCCESS
To increase on-task behaviour. To reduce the number of disputes with other pupils. To reduce the incidence of debating the boundaries with class teacher. Paul to be happier in class.	Record daily progress through the Lesson Behaviour Monitoring Sheets. On-task observations to be taken in different lessons. Disputes with other pupils to be recorded in a behaviour log.	On-task behaviour rates increase to average of 75%+. Teacher reports that Paul is not verbally challenging when she sets boundaries. Disputes with other pupils decrease. Paul reports he is happier in class.
ACTIVITIES

Programme to be based on the use of behaviour monitoring feedback sheets. (See section on Unwilling pupils.) (See appendices for example.) Daily progress to be discussed with Paul. Weekly progress to be reported to Paul's mother. | TEACHER STRATEGIES AND RESOURCES
Teacher to discuss the above targets with Paul. Paul to collect behaviour monitoring sheet each day. Teacher to negotiate rewards and sanctions with Paul. Teacher to mark a rating for how she feels about Paul's classroom progress. At the end of each session rewards or sanctions to be administered. | ORGANISATION

Each day gives a fresh start on the programme. The programme to run only so long as the bulk of the reports are positive. If it becomes an increasingly punitive programme to be discontinued (the aim is to recognise and positively reward appropriate behaviour). A contingency plan if disputes with other pupils are at a serious level or Paul continues to get marks in the sanction zone. Paul is then to go and work in the class next door. A pack of holding operation activities to be kept prepared for the use of the contingency plan. |

ACTION AT HOME
This plan was discussed with Mrs Linforth. Each day she is to discuss Paul's progress with him. She is to ring at the end of each week to discuss progress with Paul's teacher. Paul to be praised if the reports of progress he has given are largely accurate.

PASTORAL CARE AND/OR MEDICAL REQUIREMENTS
Head teacher to act as the point of referral if Paul becomes uncooperative. Also regular positive reports to head teacher to be used as an incentive if Paul is making good progress.

POSSIBLE REVIEW OUTCOMES: Continue this Stage 2 plan, move to Stage 3, move back to Stage 1.
REVIEW DECISION

Signature .... *Date* ....

Figure 15 – Individual Education Plan at Stage 2

NAME OF CHILD: David Butler	DOB: 23.5.1983	Class/yr group: 7 JS
DATE OF ACTION: 21.4.96	REVIEW DATE: 20.9.96	
SUPPORT SERVICES INVOLVED: EWO, EP, Learning Support Service		

NATURE OF CONCERN

David has had poor attendance since starting secondary school. Three programmes have been set up involving parents, EWO and year head. Currently he is escorted into school by mother but often runs away. This IEP follows intervention by the EP where the underlying problem was identified as panic attacks.

TARGETS	MONITORING	CRITERIA FOR SUCCESS
To increase the number of lessons which David completes. To increase David's ability to talk through his problems. To increase the number of days that David attends school. To improve David's confidence.	Form tutor to keep a record of the number of times David uses the contingency plan. David to keep a record card to be signed by subject teachers when he successfully completes a lesson.	Initially: David successfully uses the contingency plan and increases the number of lessons he has completed. This to be compared against records for week ending.

ACTIVITIES	TEACHER STRATEGIES AND RESOURCES	ORGANISATION
David to be involved in the normal routine of the school. If he feels a panic attack coming on he is allowed to go to the secretaries' offices where he can stay working quietly on basic literacy and number activities until the next lesson. Whenever David uses the contingency plan he is to meet at the end of the school day with his form tutor to talk through the problem: year head to offer support and supervision to secretary and form tutor to ensure the contingency plan does not become too demanding (see Panic Control, Anxious Pupils).	Form tutor to base interview after the use of contingency plan on points in booklet provided by the EP. The aim is to help David gain control in place of panic reaction. A four-point interview to follow each use of the plan and be recorded. (The fact of the interview not the detail of it.) 1) What was David thinking just before he left the lesson? 2) What happened? 3) What alternative ways could he have thought through the situation? (Teacher to model possible answers if necessary.) 4) What might have happened with a different way of thinking about the situation?	This plan arose from a meeting between all of the staff directly involved, the EP and the EWO. Year head and EP met with David and his mother separately to discuss the plan with them. Further action to be taken: 1) All staff to be briefed on the plan at next full staff meeting. 2) A printed copy of the plan to be put on the reverse of David's report sheet to ensure that David can present it to staff when moving about the school. 3) Subject teacher to sign report form only when David completes a lesson. 4) Form tutor and subject teachers to liaise regularly to ensure the system does not get corrupted. 5) Year head, form tutor and secretary to meet weekly to ensure the plan does not become too burdensome.

ACTION AT HOME

Parents to ring school each week to monitor progress. Parents to talk about each school day and praise progress made. Parents to ring school if David is refusing to go to school and EWO will respond quickly.

PASTORAL CARE AND/OR MEDICAL REQUIREMENTS

David experiences asthma attacks. Inhaler is held in the school medical room. A 10-15 minute weekly meeting to be set up between David and his form tutor to discuss progress.

POSSIBLE REVIEW OUTCOMES

Remain at Stage 3 with current programme, change Stage 3 programme or move to Stage 4.
REVIEW DECISION

Signature .... *Date* ....

Figure 16 – Individual Education Plan at Stage 3

Step two: data collection

What baseline and monitoring data do you intend collecting: Learning? Peer interactions? Teacher interactions? Events? Remember to set a period after which you will gather further information on a regular basis. Who will do this? This will need to be laid out on some form of standard record sheet.

Step three: possible explanations

While there are always many possible explanations, you are looking for those that will support useful strategies that can be applied within school.

- Are the circumstances intolerable for the pupil?

- Is the pupil unable?

- Is the pupil unwilling?

- Is the pupil unhappy?

- Is the pupil anxious?

Step four: long-term aims

While we will always be intending to remove any emotional and behavioural barriers to learning there will also be long-term improvements in the pupil's observable behaviour:

AIM 1	Learning related
AIM 2	Behavioural related

Step five

List the short-term objectives and the strategies to be used.

Key targets

Look for those changes that would lead to some immediate improvement. These are like leverage points: if you can get the right one the entire thing will start moving. For example, a pupil's out-of-seat behaviour may be a major headache to peers and class teacher. If the time the pupil stays in their seat can be increased then the other problems will decrease.

Make your target SMART: **S**pecific and small
Measurable
Achievable
Realistic
Timed over an agreed period of time

(Lloyd and Berthelot, 1992)

Step six: strategy plan

1. Who will do what in what circumstances?

2. What records will be kept?

3. Who will take responsibility?

4. Who needs to know about the plan?

Step seven: monitoring and evaluation

1. What will be the review by date?

2. What are our minimum expectations?

3. Who needs to be involved in the review?

4. When should we stop our behaviour programme?

Chapter 5 – Sanctions and Exclusions

Overall this book is about the application of positive methods to problem behaviours. In general the use of positive rewards to encourage appropriate behaviours is the most effective way of changing pupil behaviour. It is necessary, however, to consider the use of appropriate sanctions to maintain reasonable order in class and school. The following principles upon which to base generally agreed policies of sanctions are suggested in the circulars on *EBD* and *School Discipline*, DfEE 8/94; 9/94.

1. They should be applied fairly and consistently.

2. They should not undermine the child's sense of responsibility or self-respect.

3. They should complement the school's ethos of structure and order.

4. They should be encompassed in a written statement of policy.

5. They should be communicated clearly to pupils, parents, teachers, ancillary staff, governors.

6. Corrective measures should be logged.

7. They should take account of the pupil's age, understanding, disability.

(See also the section in Chapter 3 on natural and logical consequences.)

Many children who present emotional and behavioural difficulties have had poor experience of the application of reasonable sanctions. Many will have continued to cross behavioural boundaries despite the application of sanctions. Some will have experienced the impact of harsh or even abusive disciplinary regimes in their lives. It is necessary therefore for teachers to have a clear idea of the sanctions they have at their fingertips. Often the argument is promoted that schools have few sanctions which they can apply. When used effectively class teachers have at their discretion a wide range of factors which contribute to good classroom order:

- the ability to choose the content of the work for the pupils;

- the choice of the style of presentation of the work;

- the allocation of seating arrangements;

- the allocation of individual attention to the children;

- the application of appropriate eye contact;

- the ability to put additional work demands on the pupil (lines, essays etc.);

- the ability to call parents in to discuss the pupil's achievements;

- the ability to call parents in to discuss the pupil's misdemeanors;

- the ability to celebrate achievements;

- the ability to set learning targets;

- the ability to enthuse;

- the right to approve and disapprove;

- the right to exclude children;

- the right to withdraw privileges;

- the right to require pupils to keep within certain geographical bounds (i.e. pupil to stay in at break times, or pupil is denied access to lunch time clubs etc.).

Some of these can be seen as sanctions and some the use of the relationship which the teacher has established with the child. All disciplined relationships rely on the subtle use of a variety of 'carrot and stick' approaches from nursing to membership of football teams. In the school situation the use of the 'stick' element of this approach needs careful thought. The ultimate sanction is exclusion from school and all sanctions need to be geared to maintaining the enormity of that act. If the regime of sanctions in a school makes exclusion an attractive proposition then the overall disciplinary regime could be undermined by such a devaluation.

Punishment as a strategy needs also to be carefully thought about because it can elicit behaviours from the child which are maladaptive to school:

- lying to avoid punishment;

- excessive timidity;

- avoidance and even school refusal;

- teaching the lesson that 'might is right' and the correct response to undesirable behaviour is to punish it (this raises lots of questions about intolerance and could contribute to an environment which encourages bullying).

Evidence indicates that school disciplinary regimes differ widely. The behavioural response from the pupils to those regimes does not respond directly to their punitive nature or otherwise (Reynolds, 1976). It is not the case that the stricter a school is the better behaved the pupils are. The factors which seem to be more important in maintaining good discipline are:

- the overall ethos of the school;

- the likelihood of being caught for an offence which is conditioned by:
  - the movement of pupils about the school
  - the organisational arrangements
  - the geography of the school site
  - whether teachers challenge misbehaviour
  - whether they challenge the same misbehaviour;

- the extent to which the pupils concur with the code of ethics of the school;

- the extent to which parents concur with the disciplinary code of the school;

- the way in which the disciplinary code is communicated to the pupils;

- the way different members of the school community respect each other.

Sanctions seem to be at their optimum when they are proportionate to the act, are aimed at the unacceptable behaviour and not at the child, respect the dignity of the child (i.e. are non-abusive), and are timed so that the punishment is associated with the behaviour and not some time afterwards. Disciplinary regimes should promote the idea of the school being hard on issues and soft on people.

Physical restraint

This is a very sensitive subject and increases in sensitivity the farther along the continuum of behavioural difficulties under consideration. For classroom teachers in mainstream schools the issue of restraint is easier to deal with than in special school environments. Where a child is presenting regular need for restraint then they should be considered as presenting special educational needs at Stages 4 or 5 of the *Code of Practice* recommendations. There is an important consideration for the teacher in deciding what behaviour 'requires' the use of restraint, what behaviour requires assistance from a colleague or the head teacher. *Circular 9/94* gives some guidance on the issue of restraint:

Teachers may be forgiven for feeling as though they are in a situation where they are damned if they do and damned if they don't.

A general policy of no physical intervention may in general safeguard the child and the teacher from allegations of assault. It is not acceptable, however, to allow a child to harm themselves or others or cause serious physical damage to the property while the teacher stands by wringing their hands, saying 'well, what can you do?' Teachers have a duty of care for their pupils and must exercise this responsibly. It is important that a teacher feels personally secure in intervening in any situation. If they do not then they should call for help.

A confrontation with a child is not intrinsically bad but it must be like Princes Street in Edinburgh.
Robert Laslett (Lecturer in Special Education University of Birmingham)

When asked what he meant by the above statement Laslett replied that if you stood at one end of Princes Street you could see all the way to the other end. When entering into any physical restraint it is important for the teacher to be confident of the outcome from the start.

In addition it may help to consider the following questions in relation to the use of restraint.

1. What are the safety implications in a given situation:
    Is it safe to restrain a pupil?
    Is it safe not to?

2. Am I acting in anger or using restraint as a reasonable response to the situation?

3. Can I call upon other members of staff to help?

4. What will be the impact on the rest of the pupils of my actions?

5. Can I justify my actions to the child concerned, their parents, other colleagues, myself?

6. Am I physically capable of restraining the pupil concerned?

7. Does the school have contingency plans when restraint is not an option?

8. Have I used appropriate strategies to de-escalate the situation:
    - What tone of voice am I using?
    - What hand gestures am I using?
    - What is my wider body language?
    - Does my position in the classroom inhibit the child from making a flight response and therefore heighten the possibility of a fight response?
    - Am I assertive but not aggressive?

It is very important that the school supports teachers who have been involved in a restraint situation. Teachers will always have an emotional response to the event even if they are tempted to use the defense mechanism of denial of stressful feelings.

Schools which generate supportive environments in such situations will show the following:

• Are there school contingency plans for such an event? It may happen very infrequently but it is important that teachers know what procedure to follow after such an event.

• Whom should they inform?

• Where should the event be logged?

• What follow-up will take place with the pupil?

• How will parents be involved?

> Above all the teacher needs to address the question, is it my intention to prevent the child from a behaviour which is harmful to them or others or is it my intention to force the child to comply with my wishes? Physical restraint is acceptable in the first and not the second.

Physical restraint should always be a last resort. For schools which face a lot of challenging behaviour the organisational ethos needs to be addressed to avoid any drift towards increased use of physical force:

Unfortunately the ethos of some schools, day centres and other establishments do not acknowledge that some pupils will be uncooperative and, consequently, dependence on routines which rely on physical force continues. One of the painful although beneficial effects of the implementation of 'Permissible Forms of Control' (Department of Health, 1993) must be to encourage staff to meet the challenge of very difficult children more creatively.

Hewitt and Arnott (1996)

Exclusion

This term refers to the temporary or permanent withdrawal of the right to attend school. At the time of writing this book school exclusion is a topical issue. By 1996 permanent exclusions from schools had reached more than 12,000 per year and all indications were that the figure would go on rising for some time to come. The reasons for the increase are many and varied. Parsons and Howlett (1996) identified four main factors contributing to the increase in exclusions:

• Psycho-social problems are increasing and there are more behaviourally difficult children as a result.

• Family problems include an increase in poverty and family breakdown. Social problems reflect high youth unemployment and resultant alienation.

• Educational resources are stretched: schools acting as small businesses experience tension between the business and the professional ethic. Where the former prevails schools may be tempted to exclude those pupils who impede the productive enterprise.

• There is a particular cultural response to difficult undisciplined behaviour that confers blame upon the perpetrator. Excluded pupils become the culprits not the victims. Pupils with difficult behaviour are not perceived as having special needs.

A recent Economic and Social Research Council Report into exclusions from primary school identified the conditions in *Figure 17* likely to be prevalent in pupil exclusions.

The regulations governing exclusions are detailed in *Circular 10/94* at the time of writing this book. Clearly defined procedures are laid down for schools about the process of exclusion, detailing:

• the roles of head teachers and governors in the process of exclusion;

• what time limits must be put on an exclusion;

• model procedures including who must be informed and the processes involved in informing interested parties: parents, governors, the pupil;

• the rights of parents to appeal against an exclusion.

Given that these procedures are likely to change in the future it would not be helpful in this book to detail the current procedure. However, in *Circular 10/94* the guiding principles which have applied since the *Education Act 1944* are listed.

1. Head teachers should keep to a minimum the occasions on which they exclude a child from school.

2. Exclusions should only be carried out by the head teacher or the deputy acting in the absence of the head teacher.

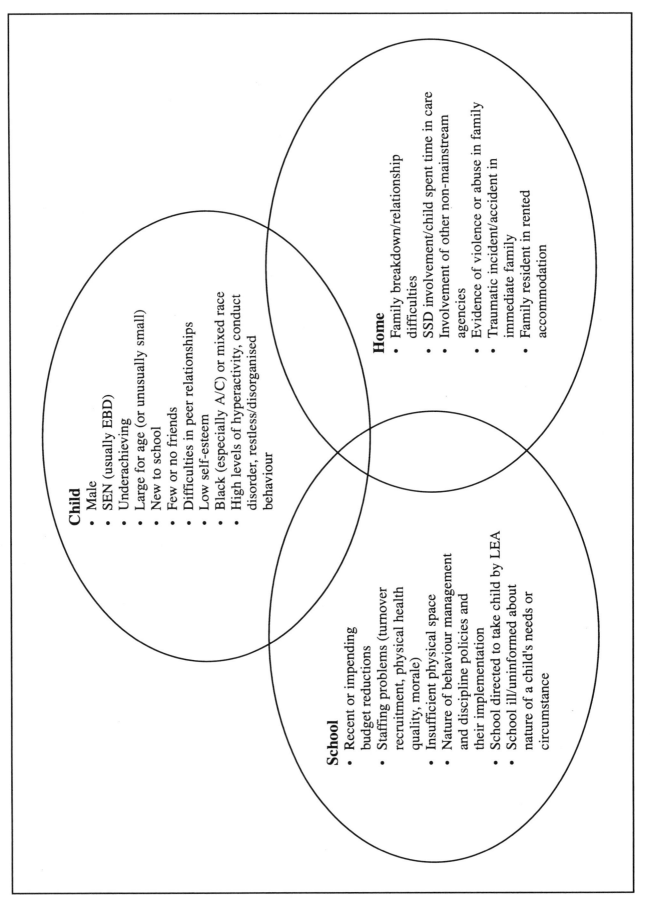

Child
- Male
- SEN (usually EBD)
- Underachieving
- Large for age (or unusually small)
- New to school
- Few or no friends
- Difficulties in peer relationships
- Low self-esteem
- Black (especially A/C) or mixed race
- High levels of hyperactivity, conduct disorder, restless/disorganised behaviour

Home
- Family breakdown/relationship difficulties
- SSD involvement/child spent time in care
- Involvement of other non-mainstream agencies
- Evidence of violence or abuse in family
- Traumatic incident/accident in immediate family
- Family resident in rented accommodation

School
- Recent or impending budget reductions
- Staffing problems (turnover recruitment, physical health quality, morale)
- Insufficient physical space
- Nature of behaviour management and discipline policies and their implementation
- School directed to take child by LEA
- School ill/uninformed about nature of a child's needs or circumstance

Figure 17 – Common variables in the characteristics and circumstances of primary school children excluded from school (Taken from: 'Exclusive Education', Children Excluded from Primary Schools, Carol Hayden, December 1996, Economic and Social Research Council).

3. Exclusion should only be in response to serious breaches of the school's policy on behaviour or of the criminal law.

4. All schools should have effective policies on behaviour.

5. The Secretary of State would expect that in each case of permanent exclusion the following would pertain:
   i) all other reasonable steps have been taken to avoid excluding the child;
   ii) allowing the child to remain in school would be seriously detrimental to the education or welfare of the pupil, or to that of others in school.

Exclusion should not be seen as a cure to a problem. There are many other things to consider when an exclusion takes place:

1. What is the likely impact on the child?

2. How do parents perceive what has happened? Damaging hostility to the school can be engendered if the reasons for the exclusion are inadequately explained to parents. While co-operation cannot be guaranteed from parents it is always helpful in the long run to explain carefully all the measures that have been take to avoid the exclusion and the reasons for deciding to exclude despite the measures.

3. What is the impact on the staff group? Do they perceive fairness in the process of exclusion?

4. How does exclusion affect the wider pupil community? Will another child step into the breach of 'most disruptive child'? Will the school be considering another exclusion shortly?

5. How does exclusion affect the wider community?

6. If the exclusion is temporary, what conditions will be established for the pupil's return?

7. If the exclusion is permanent, how will the next school, or tutorial unit (pupil referral unit) be helped to settle the pupil into a new pattern of schooling?

8. What can be learnt from the process?

9. What would be the consequences of not excluding?

It is unlikely that schools will ever get to the situation where they have sufficient support available to avert the need for any pupil exclusions. It is therefore likely to be the case that schools will need procedures available for those pupils who are disaffected or hostile. The pressure exerted by parents upon schools to ensure that their children are not subject to assault, inappropriate sexual behaviour or drug misuse will play heavily upon head teachers and governors when they make decisions. Exclusion should be a last resort but when necessary it should be done decisively, paying regard to the school policies and the pupil's well-being. (Exclusions also form part of the discussions of current and future debate in Chapter 8.)

Chapter 6 – Statutory Assessment

Movement to Stage 4 of the *Code of Practice* requires the school to take a careful look at the programme they have been offering to the child and the evidence they have assembled about the problem behaviours. A decision to instigate Stage 4 of the *Code of Practice* recommendations (Statutory Assessment in accordance with the provisions of the *Education Act 1994*) is taken by the LEA in response to:

• the length of time that concerns have existed;

• the resistance to change in response to formal programmes;

• indications that the child needs significant support to meet their needs;

• the seriousness of the behaviours under consideration;

• detailed intervention from other professionals has been sought and followed up by the school.

Many LEAs have drawn up detailed criteria for movement to Stage 4. They will ask for evidence in relation to the above. *Code of Practice* section 3.68 lists the sort of evidence that should be provided by schools, i.e. one or more of the following:

1. significant discrepancy between recorded scores of cognitive ability and classroom achievements;

2. the child is unusually withdrawn or experiences difficulties in relationships with peers or adults;

3. there is evidence of severely impaired social interaction or communication or a significantly restricted repertoire of activities, interests and imaginative development (significant concern in this area could indicate that the child is showing difficulties in the areas identified as the 'Triad of Impairment' that suggests autistic spectrum disorder (NAS 1995);

4. irregular patterns of school attendance;

5. clear recorded evidence of eating disorder;

6. recorded evidence of substance or alcohol abuse;

7. unpredictable, bizarre, obsessive, violent or severely disruptive behaviour;

8. experience of bullying as victim or perpetrator; neglect and/or abuse at home or major difficulties at home;

9. a suspicion that the child may have a significant mental health problem through sudden unpredictable changes in the child's behaviour but which may indicate the possibility of neurological impairment, e.g. epilepsy or other physical cause.

The above list is indicative and not exhaustive. Essentially if the teacher is concerned about the child's progress and feels that non-specific behavioural difficulties are at the root of their difficulties, it is important to gather evidence of the nature of the behaviour, in what circumstances it occurs, the impact it has on the child and the impact it has on the social network of the classroom. We have already alluded to the strategies that the teacher can use to gather and record such evidence.

> It cannot be stressed enough that gathering evidence about the nature and incidence of the behaviour, except in extreme circumstances, will not be enough. The evidence must show how the child has responded to the school's interventions.

Before detailing that advice it is worth commenting that the majority of emotional and behavioural difficulties emerge and subside without any specific intervention aimed at them. There is also no definite data that you can establish to say that a problem behaviour or pattern of behaviours lessened because of the intervention undertaken. It may be that the child has adjusted their behaviour for very different reasons. A list of possible reasons for spontaneous remission of problem behaviour might be:

1. your overall relationship with the child has settled down;

2. the child has changed through maturation;

3. you have changed with your knowledge of the strengths and weaknesses of the child;

4. the child's home circumstances have changed;

5. the dynamics of the class group have changed;

6. the child learns more and becomes less anxious about the classroom situation.

There is every good reason therefore to take a positive approach to the concern, to instigate a behaviour plan and to monitor progress. If the plan does not seem to be having the desired effect (the problem behaviour has continued or become more serious in its impact, or the original problem behaviour has stopped but has been replaced by more concerning behaviour) then the plan can be adjusted and further monitored. If necessary the child progresses through the *Code of Practice* stages to the point of referral to Stage 4. In such cases Section 3:69 states that schools should provide evidence in the following areas:

1. The school has sought appropriate external advice. All of the following may have a role in offering help for pupils with EBD:
    - Educational Psychologist
    - Educational Welfare Officers
    - Occupational Therapists
    - Physiotherapists
    - Speech and Language Therapists
    - the School Nurse or Medical Officer
    - Special Needs Support Service
    - Child and Adolescent Mental Health Service

    Following thorough discussions with the child and their parents, the school has formulated, implemented, monitored and evaluated IEPs, including a behaviour management programme.

2. The school has followed, as appropriate in the individual cases, the provisions of its policies on behaviour and on pastoral care and guidance.

It is very important therefore to have written policies available and to have considered how those policies are communicated to pupils, parents and staff. The principles on which any whole school behaviour policy should be built is described in DfEE *Circular 8/94, Pupil Behaviour and Discipline*. These are detailed in *Figure 18.*

- The policy should be simple and straightforward, and based on a clear and defensible set of principles or values;

- the policy should provide for the punishment of bad behaviour and encourage good behaviour;

- the policy should be specific to the school;

- rules should be kept to the minimum necessary to ensure good behaviour;

- the reason for each rule should be clear; and

- wherever possible, rules should be expressed in positive constructive terms, although it should be absolutely clear what the pupils are not allowed to do.

Figure 18

3. All staff have been fully informed of the child's difficulties and a consistent approach to remedying these difficulties has been taken across the school. The use of briefing meetings for the overall plan to be conveyed to members of staff helps to ensure consistency of approach. In schools where the pupil is likely to come into contact with a range of staff it could help them to carry a report card around so that teachers can sign to recognise and compliment the pupil on the way they are working towards specific behavioural objectives. (See example in Appendix 2.) When transmitting the behaviour plan for an individual pupil the aim should be to enlist the support of the wider staff team to help the pupil reach agreed objectives. It is essential to provide such a transfer of information where a contingency plan has been agreed upon. Briefings should consist of:

    - the background of the concern and areas of strengths in the child;

- recognised zones of vulnerability for the child, e.g. 'David is likely to have difficulties when moving from classroom to classroom', or 'Sarah finds working with new teachers difficult and therefore could have problems if a supply teacher is working with her';

- the objectives set for the child;

- who is maintaining records on the child;

- who should be contacted if there is a breakdown of the plan; when the plan will be reviewed.

The aim should be to co-ordinate ways that the child can receive support. This requires:

- primarily rewarding positive progress;

- consistent messages of where the boundaries of acceptable behaviour are in the school;

- consistent messages about the consequences of unacceptable behaviour;

- reassurance to the individual teachers that they will be supported in maintaining appropriate boundaries in school and in their classroom.

4. The school has sought a constructive relationship with the child's parents/carers, encouraging them to participate in their child's education, including visiting the school on a regular basis. As discussed earlier, this can present a great challenge to the teacher and SENCO largely because of the nature of EBD.

5. The school has, where appropriate, notified and sought the involvement of the Education Welfare Service and/or the Social Services department. These can provide a further dimension of support for parents in what will most certainly be a difficult time for them. The involvement of the EWS is essential where the concern involves extended or regular absence. Social Services involvement is essential when instigating Child Protection Procedures.

6. The school has explored the possible benefits of, and where practicable secured access for the child to, appropriate information technologies as a means to motivating and stimulating the child, e.g. word processing facilities, painting programmes and other software which encourages communication and self-expression. The school should provide opportunities in the use of that technology for the child, his or her parents and staff so that the child is able to use that technology across the curriculum in school and wherever possible at home.

7. The school has, with the parents' consent, notified and sought the assistance of the school doctor and/or the child's GP, as appropriate. This can be a very important move for the child. Area health authorities or NHS Trusts must provide services for children and young people under the provisions of the *Children Act 1989*. The following services can be provided: child guidance, clinical psychologist input, family therapy, psychiatric services, counselling. Different health services have different referral routes. Some will take referrals directly from schools, some will take referrals from educational psychologists and some will only take referrals from GP or other health departments. By routing a referral to child guidance services through the child's GP, good professional practice can be maintained.

Chapter 7 – A Whole School Approach

A whole school policy is only as good as the practice it initiates, develops and sustains.
Vanessa Gordon (1989)

Throughout this book we have been attempting to provide positive approaches to problem behaviour. To be effective with such behaviour it may be possible to work effectively in isolation but generally the more cohesive and open the staff team are the more likely it is that individual teachers will feel empowered to cope with difficulties. The following features seem to be evident in teams which perform well together:

1. They have clear common goals.

2. They are open and honest with each other.

3. They focus on achieving high standards.

4. They plan well together.

5. They are flexible enough to divert from the plan to support colleagues under stress.

6. They have effective leadership. (This is a complex issue but one that is so important that it needs to be examined constantly. There appears to be no one set style of leadership that works better than all of the others. Effective leadership seems more to be an expression of the compatibility of the style of leadership with the group dynamics of the staff team and the demands of the task. Clearly the issue of leadership is so important that it is not sufficient for the school management team to ask, are we enabling the team to perform their jobs well? It is important too for every member of the staff team to ask, am I helping my manager to lead effectively?)

7. They are appropriately resourced to carry out the task:
   - Do you have appropriate physical resources?
   - Are the resources managed effectively?
   - Do you have sufficient personnel?
   - Are they managed effectively?

8. Communication is managed effectively throughout the team.

9. There are clear induction strategies which provide support at vulnerable times.

10. Achievement is recognised and celebrated.

11. The impact of special measures is regularly evaluated (see section on IEPs).

The effective team will not let a colleague become stressed in response to persistent behaviour difficulties. They will provide support which enables the staff working directly with the problem behaviours to develop their expertise. This is particularly important in relation to the classroom support assistant (CSA).

Classroom Support Assistants

Those adults who support teachers in classrooms have assumed a variety of titles. In some schools they are classroom support assistants, in others welfare assistants, sometimes they are called general assistants or, as in the HMI report referred to later in this section, special support assistants. The least complimentary title for these very underrated colleagues is non-teaching assistant. It is curious to have a job title which tells everybody what you do not do in preference to what you do. (Imagine being told that this book was being written by two non-solicitors.)

When we refer to CSAs we are referring to those people who are employed to support class teachers in providing additional help to pupils. Sometimes they will be employed to help a specific teacher and class and their role with pupils with SEN is incidental. Sometimes they will have been employed specifically to work with one particular pupil. Whichever is the case they will provide a direct influence on the quality of learning for our pupils.

The presence of another adult close to a distractible child can exert a measure of proximity control. Without careful co-ordination, the relationship between teacher, CSA and child can be fraught with difficulties. In addition to detailed planning of the input they will make with the child, e.g. help with classroom organisation, providing additional guidance and support with reading or transcribing ideas for the pupil, providing opportunities to practice skills in small groups, the CSA will need emotional support to cope with demanding behaviour etc. See Appendix 3 Managing Stress.

Classroom support assistants and lunch time supervisors can often feel isolated or singled out for bad behaviour by the pupils. They can also feel that the pupil is trying to draw them into colluding with bad behaviour against the teachers. Sometimes they can doubt the wisdom of a particular line taken by a teacher towards a particular incident with a child.

An effective team will ensure that these colleagues, who from day to day work directly with our most vulnerable children, are appropriately skilled, have access to training, receive ongoing support, and have time to plan and reflect on programmes. How effective an individual CSA is will often have a pivotal impact on even the best worked out IEP.

Rennie (1996) describes the underlying issues which need to be considered when establishing a behavioural support relationship. These are pertinent points to ponder whether that support comes from a CSA or a behavioural support teacher:

- targets for support;

- curriculum;

- roles, responsibilities and methodology;

- working links and support;

- training;

- evaluation.

Findings from HMI Survey

The need for effective teamwork was amongst the findings from the HMI Survey on SEN in Mainstream Schools (1996). The survey was carried out March-December 1994 and spanned the introduction of the *Code of Practice*. HMIs visited 33 LEAs and inspected over 140 schools. Their findings were wide and varied and referred to the whole range of SEN. In particular HMI made the following reference to joint planning.

At all key stages the most influential factor on the effectiveness of in-class support is the quality of joint planning work between class/subject teacher and the support teacher or special support assistant (SSA).

Hanko (1994) discusses the importance of joint problem solving approaches within staff teams to help understand those children who are unresponsive to positive reinforcements. Those she describes as 'discouraged children'. She emphasizes the importance of establishing a professional environment where colleagues have developed the interpersonal skills to act as 'non-judgmental critical friends' in exploring ways children relate in the classroom to find appropriate strategies to encourage them. She states:

By jointly exploring the child's learning experience from the child's perspective, they (teachers and others) are more likely to become aware of the factors that have impeded a specific child's learning and may consequently discover the most appropriate response within a classroom-focused problem solving framework.

Managing Difficult Issues: Some Survival Tips

All organisations have inherent points of conflict or tensions. As this book illustrates clearly, children with emotional and behavioural difficulties often magnify those stresses or tensions. One strong performance indicator of an effective school is its ability to turn potential conflict into creative energy.

Key questions the school may ask
- How many registered concerns and IEPs is it reasonable for a class teacher to manage?

- Do you measure the success of your responses to the *Code of Practice*? Do they rate as highly as academic achievements?

- Do you 'audit' the types of IEPs you have, to discern patterns and decide school needs and staff development?

- Is the SENCO enabled to support class/subject teachers to apply the *Code of Practice*?

- How do you actively involve and inform parents?

- How do you actively involve pupils in reviewing their own progress, setting targets etc.?

- How do you ensure that at Stage 3 your support services work collaboratively?

- How does the senior management team support your implementation of the *Code of Practice*?

Conflict Management
Sometimes it is necessary to take stock of an issue causing concern and apply a more formal conflict resolution strategy. In any such approach the general aim is always to strive to be:

Hard on issues, respectful of people.

Conflict Resolution
The aim should always be assertiveness and never aggressiveness. Do not enter into a conflict resolution unless you are prepared to give as much as receive. Know the range of outcomes which will be acceptable to you. Never agree to something which you know you cannot live with. Saying no is difficult sometimes but it is better said than picking up on the consequences later.

Not addressing the issue is seldom a conflict resolution strategy.

The 5 R's: A strategy for working with pupils, parents and colleagues
1. REFLECT ... DEFINE THE BEHAVIOUR
   Be precise. What is the behaviour you would like to address? How can you achieve a win-win situation? Avoid being judgmental; describe the behaviour, not personality traits. Use factual non-blaming description in order to reduce defensive reactions. Criticism leads to a defensive reaction, which results in inflexibility.

2. REPORT ... WHAT IS THE RESULT OF THE BEHAVIOUR?
   Seek a relaxed meeting, without time constraints or interruptions to discuss the issue with all interested parties. What is the result of the behaviours at issue? What do they cost: time? money? other? When discussing the issue be clear, precise and objective. Avoid generalisations, 'You always ...' Avoid guessing at underlying motives to explain the behaviour, 'You are thoughtless ... etc.' If you criticise someone's personality or behaviour in a general way you are likely to make them defensive and less open to change. Stay with the issue.

3. RELATE ... WHAT ARE YOUR EXPECTATIONS?
   What do you hope to achieve: a change in behaviour, more awareness, if so in what ways? What are the expectations, rules etc. in operation? Convey your desire to sort out the difficulty. Convey an understanding that others may feel strongly about this issue. Accept criticism without responding to the desire to defend yourself. Find out what expectations the other parties have in this situation.

4. REQUESTING ... WHAT IS YOUR OBJECTIVE?
   Request in concrete terms whatever you wish to see done differently. Do not plead or bargain. What you can give in this situation should be given unconditionally. Make sure your request is reasonable and within their own power. You may ask them, 'What action would you take under these circumstances if you were in my position?' or 'Can you think of any ideas which will help?' People are more likely to have a commitment to their own idea. Discuss the range of different consequences for different outcomes.

5. RESULTS
   Be clear about the positive consequences and why you need their active co-operation. If you reach an acceptable resolution, agree a time at some future date to review progress. If you fail to resolve matters, agree a time to discuss the matter further. If it is clear that it is unlikely that you will achieve a resolution, you should always know your next step. You may tell them your intended further action as a last resort.

Always ensure that in any conflict resolution you follow a cycle of:

Open discussion >>> Agreed solution >>> All parties work as hard as they can to ensure agreed solution is successful >>>> If unsuccessful: return to open discussion.

(Grove, 1987)

Debriefing

Sometimes the above strategies will go wrong in the best run establishment. The term 'crisis management' is often used in a prejudicial sense. Phrases such as 'There was an over-reliance on crisis management in the establishment' appear as criticisms in reports. It is important to remember that at times of crisis, effective management is essential. In the face of serious incidents which can sometimes result when working with children in distress, the care and concern shown by the school community is essential.

Research into traumatic events indicate that serious long-term problems can arise eventually from incidents which are not followed up systematically. In the aftermath of an accident or an assault, the victims should be treated gently and allowed time to recover ... it is tea and sympathy time. Some time afterwards, time should be set aside to discuss the incident to allow the victim to explore their feelings. It may be necessary to carry out this sort of debriefing on a number of occasions. For most moderately serious incidents (someone is assaulted and is shaken but not physically injured) a sympathetic, non-judgmental discussion within 24 hours of the event can help. This sort of debriefing can follow an informal structure which explores:

Facts: What was the sequence of events ... who did what?

Feelings: What emotions were aroused during the event? The victim should be assured that feelings of anger, fear, panic are normal and OK.

Future: What is to be done to face up to the future implications of the event?

For more serious events it is important for the school to liaise with the Educational Psychology Service, the Child and Adolescent Mental Health Services and the Social Services department to ensure that appropriate post-trauma response is proportionate and is co-ordinated.

Chapter 8 – Emotional and Behavioural Difficulties: The Current and Future Debate

Emotional and behavioural issues are always the subject of fierce debate. There is no other area of special educational needs that will elicit from intelligent adults that the only thing needed by children who behave badly is to receive 'a damned good hiding'. Such a point of view is as preposterous as the *laissez-faire* approach of the non-interventionist. While most people are in agreement about the desirability of orderly behaviour and a calm learning environment, the mechanisms which achieve this are often the subject of great disagreement. Below are some of the issues which arise in debates.

The Curriculum

This book started with the proposition that children with emotional and behavioural difficulties face barriers to learning. No consideration of the needs of children with EBD is complete without careful consideration of the curricular needs. Certainly children with EBD will most probably have missed significant sections of their basic learning. Many will have literacy and numeracy problems and will therefore need significant learning support. A number of additional questions arise in relation to the design of learning programmes for children with EBD:

1. How can we provide a broad and balanced curriculum and ensure that control over the learning environment is maintained?

2. Does the pupil have significant talents which can be built upon?

3. How much can they benefit from unsupervised learning situations, e.g. library research or field study trips, without becoming vulnerable?

4. What learning experience can be introduced to help the pupil overcome their emotional and behavioural difficulties, e.g. cognitive behavioural strategies?

5. How can the time demands of therapeutic interventions and the demands of the curriculum be reconciled?

Care and Control

This issue may affect all teachers from time to time but is especially poignant in relation to the special school population. The requirements of the *Children Act 1989* and the outcome of numerous inquiries into abuse of 'children in care' (now referred to as 'looked after' children) indicates the need for continuing vigilance over the methods used to achieve good order. Equally there is a general mood of concern about levels of discipline in society. The simple solution is for schools to turn their backs on children with difficulties. The end result of such a process is to develop increasingly difficult problems for those who become disaffected from school. Most schools have a strong commitment to all of their pupils and consider meeting the needs of vulnerable children to be a high priority. In an increasingly litigious society it is, however, clear that schools will need to constantly address the issues around caring for and controlling those children whose behaviour is challenging.

Like other issues where there are no easy solutions, there is much to be gained by considering care and control as an organisational quality issue and incorporating it as a fixed item on staff meeting agendas. It could also help to include it as a section in the school development plan. Other strategies might include the use of a focus group drawn from parents, pupils, teachers and governors. Whatever the strategy used, it should ensure that this issue is kept under regular review.

Attention Deficit Disorder

Recent years have seen the increased use by doctors and child psychiatrists of the diagnosis of ADD or ADHD. While this handbook is not the right place to fully consider this issue, it would be remiss not to address this matter at all. This is an important area for us all to have some understanding of, as we are almost certain to meet children who have this diagnosis and are on a course of medication as a result.

The term was first used in America in the 1980s to describe a syndrome observed in children with such characteristics as inattention, distractibility and impulsiveness. In the United Kingdom, it is better known as hyperactivity. When hyperactivity is not present then it is called Attention Deficit Disorder. While the onset is early, by the age of 3, it is usually later that the child is referred for professional attention, often when the child has started school, which is understandable.

Common symptoms
- *Inattention*
  The child fidgets; is careless and restless; fails to listen or complete tasks; does not follow instructions; forgets daily routines; loses essential equipment; is easily distracted.

- *Hyperactivity*
  The child runs or climbs about; finds quiet play difficult; wanders from their seat; is 'always' on the go.

- *Impulsivity*
  The child speaks out of turn; interrupts others when speaking; has difficulties waiting their turn.

Children with these difficulties are also more often found to have specific literacy difficulties and to be clumsy.

Is AD(H)D an explanation or a description?

It is immediately clear that all of the 'symptoms' of ADD/ADHD are in varying degrees common at some time to all children. A serious problem is that no single assessment tool exists which can conclusively diagnose ADD/ADHD. What happens is that information is taken from a wide range of sources, usually parents and teachers, and an evaluation is made. Not surprisingly difficulties exist in achieving consensus. Parents and teachers are commenting on children's behaviour in very different contexts. Similarly a professional 'one off' snapshot in the surgery or clinic is unreliable in providing a definite diagnosis.

It is this difficulty in diagnosing ADD/ADHD which has made it a controversial term (not dissimilar to dyslexia in many ways). We may well agree that a child has many of the difficulties as outlined above, but are these features of 'normal development' or indications of an underlying pathological condition – which requires active intervention?

What causes ADD and ADHD?

There have been many causes of ADD/ADHD put forward: genetic, environmental, perinatal, toxic, family interactions and parenting styles. Allergies have been suggested but research has failed to confirm a link. On the other hand, lead has been found to be associated with a decline in intellectual performance, attention distractibility and impulsiveness (Hinshaw, 1994).

Research is beginning to suggest that ADD/ADHD is best seen to be a general term. It probably encompasses a number of sub-groups of children who have not dissimilar symptoms. But the reasons for these symptoms are many, just as fever is a symptom common to many illnesses.

It has been estimated that some 3.5 per cent of the school population suffers from ADD/ADHD. When we have such concerns over a child's behaviour we should involve the parents/guardian and follow the *Code of Practice*. With home support it may be helpful to seek medical advice.

Support for children with ADHD

This usually follows a multi-modal approach consisting of:

- behaviour modification;

- medication;

- parent training;

- counselling.

If a child is on medication then a planning meeting with all involved will be essential to ensure good communication and an integral approach. It should be stressed that medication is not seen as a solution in itself. Instead it enables a pupil to benefit more fully from other interventions to help them regain control of their behaviour. Interventions are needed in such areas as peer relationships, control of aggression and academic achievement (Hinshaw, 1994).

School-based interventions would include programmes described throughout this book focusing on:

- structured peer activities;

- clear guidelines for behaviour with strong rewards;

- home/school reward systems;

- pupil involvement in setting goals, recording and rewards;

- role play to teach new behaviours;

- circle time to teach understanding and new skills.

- self-control skills, e.g. STOP, THINK, ACT.

Current understanding does not enable an easy account of ADD/ADHD. On the positive side it does offer a meaningful explanation for some children with severe difficulties. But many children who are passing through normal development, with short-term behavioural difficulties, will be described as having ADD/ADHD.

One danger of this will result from the focus being on the child and not on the outside circumstances which may in fact be the true cause of their difficulties. At a pragmatic level perhaps little harm will be done as the same support will generally be prescribed as for most other pupils with emotional and behavioural difficulties. This is not to say that there will not be some where their behaviour was a symptom of outside stressors, from learning, home or friendships, which will not be looked for, and the support provided is palliative and not particularly curative.

A more concerning trend will be if the only way for pupils with these difficulties to receive support is through being diagnosed as having either ADD/ADHD. Not only will this jeopardise the effective and fair use of scarce resources but it may also limit our readiness to look more widely, to factors outside of children, as possible causes for their difficulties. Furthermore the question of placing children on medication, often without the support recommended in the literature to go alongside, combined with a less than complete understanding of this 'syndrome' should give us cause for concern.

Resources

Unfortunately solutions to emotional and behavioural difficulties in school and the community rarely come cheaply. This is especially so in relation to residential or other special education but the same applies in mainstream day schools. Providing opportunities for individual or small group tuition competes with resources in other areas of the school. For the most disturbed of children there is often a tendency to take a minimalist approach to resourcing which can store up more expensive problems for later. Unfortunately the public reaction towards children with emotional and behavioural difficulties often leads to resentment of the resources given. It is imperative therefore that schools seek to establish effective monitoring procedure so that when expensive choices need to be made they are done with a clear rationale and there is some evidence to support the type of provision selected. When children are sent elsewhere as a knee-jerk reaction it often means that expensive but ineffective provision is made.

Standards

Striving to raise standards of achievement is central to the process of education. It is important in doing so to evaluate the impact of measures taken to improve standards on all children. Measures which raise standards for some at the expense of others should be seen as fundamentally flawed. When the focus is solely on exam success for the majority of children there is often increased pressure for the removal of those children who are perceived to disrupt the learning of others.

One of the challenges for the future is for schools to develop clear policies about the raising of expectations for all children including those with emotional and behavioural difficulties or other SEN. Research is currently underway into calculating 'value-added' progress for schools. The current predominant methods for measuring the raising of standards which focus on exam pass rates or progress against SATs does little to recognise the enormous efforts schools may make to hold together programmes for children with EBD. Hopefully we will attain some recognition of school's efforts through:

- the raising of attendance levels;

- the maintenance of effective learning environment;

- the use of detailed multi-professional planning;

- range of therapeutic interventions;

- lack of permanent exclusions;

- parental liaison initiatives.

Pupil Exclusions

Throughout 1996 a number of high profile cases of pupil exclusions and threats of industrial action by teachers in response to pupil behaviour hit the media headlines. Amongst the reasons stated for the assertion that teachers were facing greater difficulties in managing pupil behaviour was the impact of the closure of special schools.

There was little evidence to support this view but in numerous articles it was propounded. The assertion was given credence by the issuing of a report by the Economic and Social Research Council (1996) 'Exclusive Education' which included the view about the closure of special schools in the list of factors identified as behind the huge increase in pupil exclusions. Those factors were:

- a more competitive market-orientated school environment;

- the restrictions of the National Curriculum;

- moves to integrate children from special schools and units;

- moves away from residential education in various forms;

- broader socio-economic factors, e.g. poverty, breakdown of family, patterns of employment/unemployment.

For those in the world of special education the over-simplification of essentially very complex issues raised lots of concerns. While everyone strives to uphold the rights of teachers to teach and pupils to learn in a positive and calm environment, the processes of achieving this are not usually served through the vilification of vulnerable children.

Pupil exclusions from schools reached more than 10,000 per year in 1996 and look set to continue to rise. The debate so far has often failed to address the wider issues listed above and has concentrated on those few children who received but did not benefit from a short-lived notoriety. This presents concerns about what happens to the child once they have been excluded from school. For every excluded child there are a wide variety of issues for the local neighbourhood to solve. Inevitably the situation will be solved by attention to the wider issues which have brought about increased disaffection from school.

Whole School Behaviour Packages
(Beware of the call of the snake-oil salesman)

There are a number of whole school approaches on the market, e.g. Assertive Discipline. These involve the whole staff team in drawing up detailed plans to govern disciplinary procedures. Paradoxically these approaches sometimes seem to work best where they are least needed. Where the staff team are receptive to new ideas, plan well together and work hard to implement joint plans, these approaches can be an enormous asset to development. Where rivalry exists, where colleagues compete with each other or stand in judgment of each other, where empires are built and defended, where individuals do not implement joint action plans, then such measures are more likely to be ineffective.

The implementation of a new way of working is fraught with dangers. Books like *The Myth of the Hero Innovator* suggest that the change process is complex and relates strongly to the culture of an organisation. Before considering the introduction of quick fix measures, a good deal of work needs to be undertaken to ensure that the team will be receptive to the programme and that adequate measures are available to maintain its usage once it is in operation. The best way of ensuring that process takes place is a process of decision making which follows the cycle detailed at the end of the section on Conflict Resolution.

School Inspection

The OFSTED framework lists one of the indicators of poor match between teaching and pupils' learning as poor pupil behaviour. This has led to a position where there is far more written about the 'deficiencies' identified in dealing with problem behaviour than there is in describing models of good practice. Moreover it is difficult to identify models of good practice from the special school sector where it might be expected that the best expertise is located. There has been considerable concern, however, about the number of special schools for children with EBD that get poor inspection reports. Often the reason for the criticism was evidence of bad behaviour among the pupils. This is a trend often surprisingly found. After all, schools for children with sensory impairment do not get criticised because their children have visual or auditory difficulties. The result is that good models of practice have been hard to find.

For teachers, especially head teachers, governors and LEAs the punishment for a bad OFSTED report is severe. School rolls may fall as parents seek the 'good' school for their child. Head teachers can lose their jobs. Governors can be pilloried in the press. Inevitably class teachers feel vulnerable if they are being inspected where there is a persistently disruptive (damaged) child in the classroom. At times of inspection clear contingency plans should be in place to support the class teacher where they have such difficulties.

There have been a number of undoubted benefits from the inspection process. A positive report with a number of points to address can be a very useful planning tool for any staff team. Also the process of regular inspections means that schools cannot sink into the deep malaise that sadly affected a minority of schools in the past who so badly served their pupils. The benefits need to be viewed, however, against some of the issues raised above.

Inclusion and Integration

While there have been some moves towards the integration of children with SEN generally, the number of children in special schools has only reduced slightly. While the issues surrounding the integration of a child with physical or sensory difficulties may be relatively straightforward, there are more complex difficulties in relation to EBD. Because of the nature of their difficulties the school needs to address:

- the impact of the integration on the child concerned;

- the follow-up support available (schools will be more willing to take part in integration programmes which are well supported and less willing where the converse is true);

84

- the impact of the integration on other children;

- the impact on the balance of the school community.

The most successful integration programmes are built on careful planning of the support procedures and the contingencies to be used when things do not go according to plan.

This book has focused on the development of strategies for pupils at Stage 1 to 3 of the *Code of Practice*. Inevitably there will be some pupils in mainstream schools who have statements of SEN for emotional and behavioural difficulties. Whether mainstream school is appropriate for those children can only be decided in relation to their difficulties.

Our guiding principle is encompassed in the words of Micheline Mason,

In the end it is only relationships which matter or which give our lives meaning. This is why I believe a 'special' segregated education system is so harmful to society because it depends for its existence on the breaking of relationships. An inclusive education system will have to rate friendship at least as highly as spelling. Then we will be appalled at how little we know or understand about each other.

Special vs. Mainstream

Making a decision to seek a special school placement needs to be considered very carefully. There will be some children for whom attendance in a local school is very problematic. Disputes may have occurred in the local neighbourhood and then been taken into school, presenting intolerable stresses on the child. Moreover some children refuse to attend their local schools. In the first instance an alternative mainstream placement should be chosen. A number of mainstream school placements may have proved unsuccessful, however.

For such children the easy answer might be to consider special school placement. This needs to be considered against the possible impact of placing a child with emotional and behavioural difficulties alongside a number of other children with exactly the same difficulties. There are no easy answers to this conundrum.

Decisions must be taken with the best interests of the child as paramount. In order to make the right decision a detailed understanding of the child's needs and their strengths should be weighed against the possible benefits of a range of different placement options. It is important to know what we are seeking to achieve for the pupil and their parents and to assess rigorously whether a proposed placement is likely to increase or decrease the likelihood of meeting their needs. Alongside such a projection a thorough risk assessment should be conducted in relation to any proposed placement.

Final Comment

Children with emotional and behavioural difficulties present enormous challenges. This book has tried to reflect an awareness of those difficulties and show empathy for the class teacher in facing them. It needs to be stated, however, as a parting gesture, that making progress with a child who has experienced emotional and behavioural difficulties can be an uplifting, rewarding and professionally enhancing experience. As we look back through our careers, it is those children who presented difficulties but who were won round by the application of gentle, caring, good teaching that stick in our memories.

There are also compelling reasons to work hard for our most vulnerable youngsters which impact on the ethos of our classrooms and schools generally:

1. The positive management of pupils' behaviour through attention to: the structure of lessons, effective preparation and appropriate differentiation benefits all pupils.

2. The establishment of clear ground rules for pupil behaviour creates a secure learning environment for all teachers and pupils alike.

3. Clear attention to behavioural strategies will help to protect the rights of all teachers to teach and pupils to learn. Decisions to exclude children will only be taken as extreme measures and alternatives will be sought for those children who cannot cope in a mainstream setting. Thus protection is increased for the most vulnerable children.

4. There will be a reduction in stress for teachers and a willingness to ask for help when it is needed and give help without blame when necessary. Both the asking and the giving will be seen as normal events in school.

5. As the effectiveness in tackling behaviour increases, schools will be more confident that behaviour can change.

6. In safe environments children who exhibit behavioural problems will feel safe enough to show their softer and, to them, more vulnerable qualities. It will be possible to see good in a wider range of pupils.

7. Schools can be seen as resources for the whole community if they can change the behaviour of those on the periphery of society.

8. The most vulnerable parent will be able to see hope in their children.

9. The aim of creating schools for all will be ever closer to becoming a reality.

In short the strategies we adopt to ensure educational progress for those children presenting management difficulties will enhance the provision we make for all children. Or perhaps that should read: the more effective the strategies we use to help all of our children achieve in their education, the more effective we will become in responding to children with emotional and behavioural difficulties.

The school which makes effective provision for children with emotional and behavioural difficulties is just like any other school only more so.

Jonathan Fogell and Rob Long with thanks to a Brighton head teacher

---

References and Further Reading

Alsop, P and McCaffrey, T (1993) *How to Cope with Childhood Stress: A Practical Guide for Teachers.* Longman.

Barkley, R A (1990) *Attention-Deficit Hyperactivity Disorder.* The Guildford Press.

Barkley, R A (1987) *Defiant Children.* The Guildford Press.

Barrett, M and Trevitt (1991) *Attachment Behaviour and the Schoolchild.* Tavistock/Routledge.

Besag, V (1992) *We don't have bullies here!* Besag.

Brigham, T (1989) *Self Management for Adolescents.* The Guildford Press.

Charlton, T and David, K (eds.) (1989) *Managing Misbehaviour.* Macmillan.

Chazan, M, Laing, Davies (1994) *Emotional and Behaviour Difficulties in Middle Childhood.* The Falmer Press.

Cowie, H and Pecherek, A (1994) *Counselling Approaches and Issues in Education.* David Fulton.

Creemers, B P (1994) *The Effective Classroom.* Cassell.

Dearing, R (1994) *The National Curriculum and Its Assessment.* SCAA.

Department of Health (1995) *A Handbook on Child and Adolescent Mental Health.* HMSO and DfEE.

Department of Health (1993) *Permissible Forms of Control in Children's Residential Care.*

Docking, J (ed.) (1990) *Education and Alienation in the Junior School.* The Falmer Press.

Elliot, M (1991) *Bullying: a practical guide to coping for schools.* Longman.

Elton, Lord (1989) *Discipline in Schools: Report of the Committee of Enquiry.* HMSO.

Farrell, P (ed.) (1995) *Children with Emotional and Behavioural Difficulties.* The Falmer Press.

Fogell, J (1996) From Strength to Strength: uses of solution focussed work as an LEA educational psychologist, *Special! Summer 1996.* NASEN.

Fontana, D (1994) *Managing Classroom Behaviour.* BPS.

Gold, Y and Roth, R (1993) *Teachers Managing Stress.* The Falmer Press.

Goleman, D (1996) *Emotional Intelligence.* Bloomsbury.

Gordon, V (1989) *Your Primary School: Your Policy for Special Educational Needs.* NASEN.

Graham, P and Hughes, C (1995) *So Young So Sad So Listen.* Gaskell/West London Health Promotion Agency.

Greenhalgh, P (1994) *Emotional Growth and Learning.* Routledge.

Grove, A S (1987) 'Decisions Decisions', in Organ, D (ed.) *The Applied Psychology of Work Behaviour 3rd Edition.* Business Publications (Texas).

Hanko, G (1994) 'Discouraged Children: when praise does not help', in *British Journal of Special Education, Vol. 21 No. 4.* NASEN.

Harrington, R (1993) *Depressive Disorder in Childhood and Adolescence.* Wiley.

Hayden, C (1996) *Children Excluded from School: Policies and Practices in England and Wales.* Economic and Social Research Council.

Herbert, M (1993) *Working with Children and the Children Act.* BPS.

Hewitt, D and Arnett, A (1996) 'Guidance on the use of physical force by staff in educational establishments', in *British Journal of Special Education, Vol. 23 No. 3.* NASEN.

Hill, J (1994) *Person-Centred Approaches in Schools.* PCCS Books.

Hinshaw, S P (1994) *Attention Deficits and Hyperactivity in Children.* Sage.

HMI/Audit Commission (1989) *Getting in on the Act.* HMSO.

Holmes, T H and Rahe, R H (1967) The Social Readjustment Rating Scale, *The Journal of Psychosomatic Research,* II, 213-218.

Jewett (1982) *Helping Children Cope with Separation and Loss.* B T Batsford Ltd.

Laslett, R (1977) *Educating Maladjusted Children.* Granada Publishing.

Lesotho, J and Howard-Rose, D (1994) *Anger in the Classroom.* Detselig Enterprises Ltd.

Lethem, J (1994) *Moved to tears, moved to action.* BT Press.

Lloyd, S R and Berthelot, C (1992) *Self-Empowerment: How to get what you want from life.* Kogan Page.

London (1964) quote taken from Palmer, S and Dryden, W (1995) *Counselling for Stress Problems.* Sage.

Mabey, J and Sorensen, B (1995) *Counselling For Young People.* Oxford University Press.

Maher and Zins (1987) *Psycho-educational Interventions in the School.* Pergamon Press.

Maines, B and Robinson, G (1993) *The No Blame Approach.* Lucky Duck Publishing.

McGuiness, J (1993) *Teacher, Pupils and Behaviour: A Managerial Approach.* Cassell.

Mason, M (undated) *Images of a Movement (Liberty Equality Disability) No. 4.* Leeds Postcards.

National Autistic Society (1995) *Could This Be Autism?* NAS.

OFSTED (1996) *Promoting High Achievement: For pupils with special educational needs in mainstream schools.* HMSO.

O'Hagan (1994) *Emotional and Psychological Abuse of Children.* Oxford University Press.

Oster, G (1995) *Helping Your Depressed Teenager.* John Wiley and Sons.

Parsons, C and Howlett, K (1996) 'Permanent exclusions from school: A case where society is failing its children,' in *Support for Learning, Vol. 11 No. 3.* NASEN.

Rennie (1993) in *Support for Learning, Vol. 8 No. 1.* NASEN.

Reynolds, D (1976) 'The Delinquent School', in Hammersley M, et al. *The Process of Schooling.* Routledge Kegan Paul.

Robertson, J (1989) *Effective Classroom Control.* Hodder and Stoughton.

Roe, M (1978) in Gillham, W (ed.) *Reconstructing Educational Psychology.* Croom Helm.

Rutter, M and Smith, D J (1995) *Psychosocial Disorders in Young People.* Wiley.

Selekman, M D (1993) *Pathways to Change.* The Guildford Press.

Slaby, A and Garfinkel, L F (1994) *No One Saw My Pain: Why teens kill themselves.* W W Norton and Company.

Smith, H (1996) *Procedures, Practice and Guidance for SENCOs.* NASEN.

Smith, H (1995) *Unhappy Children: Reasons and Remedies.* Free Association Books.

Smith, P K and Thompson, D A (eds.) (1991) *Practical Approaches to Bullying.* David Fulton.

Thompson, C and Rudolph, L B (1992) *Counselling Children.* Brooks/Cole Publishing Company.

Underwood Report (1955) *Report of the Committee on Maladjusted Children.* HMSO.

Varma, V (1993) *Management of Behaviour in Schools.* Longman.

Varma, V (1993) *How and Why Children Fail.* Jessica Kingsley Publishers.

Varma, V (ed.) (1993) *Coping with Unhappy Children.* Cassell.

Varma, V (ed.) (1992) *The Secret Life of Vulnerable Children.* Routledge.

Warnock, H M (1978) *Special Educational Needs: The Report of The Committee of Inquiry into the Education of Handicapped Children and Young People.* HMSO.

Webb, N B (1993) *Helping Bereaved Children.* The Guildford Press.

Wilson, D and Newton, C (1996) A Circle of Friends, in *Special Children,* January 1996. Questions Publishing.

Winkley, L (1996) *Emotional Problems in Children and Young People.* Cassell.

Useful Addresses

Advisory Centre for Education ACE
1B Aberdeen Studios, 22-24 Highbury Grove, London N5 2EA

Association of Workers for Children with EBD
Charlton Court, East Sutton, Maidstone, Kent ME17 3DQ

The Brief Therapy Practice
4d Warwick Court, Shirland Mews, London W9 1DY

The Child Psychotherapy Trust
21 Maresfield Gardens, London NW3 5SH

Contact a Family (CAF)
170 Tottenham Court Road, London W1

CRUSE Bereavement Care
Cruse House, 126 Sheen Road, Richmond, Surrey TW9 1UR

IPSEA
Independent Panel of Special Education Advisers, 22 Warren Hill Road, Woodbridge, Suffolk IP12 4DU

Kidscape
152 Buckingham Palace Road, London W1

National Autistic Society
276 Willesden Lane, London NW2 5RB

NASEN
NASEN House, 4/5 Amber Business Village, Amber Close, Amington, Tamworth B77 4RP

The Rathbone Society (support for pupils with Moderate Learning Difficulties)
The Excalibur Building, 77 Whitworth Street, Manchester M1 6EZ

Appendix 1 – On-Task Behaviour Record

General Considerations

The on-task behaviour is a flexible observation record which gives quantifiable data about the child's progress in one lesson. One single observation will give information which is useful to a class teacher. It is, however, a snapshot of behaviour which may inform judgments about the sort of concerns a particular child presents. More detailed information will come from a number of separate classroom observations and these can give useful evidence about patterns of behaviour, support needs, evaluation of the effectiveness of programmes and a range of other information.

Directions

This intervention should be carried out by an observer who is not normally a part of the focus lesson. It is not practicable for a teacher to teach and carry out this detailed observation at the same time. It is equally impracticable for a classroom support assistant who is normally part of the focus lesson to carry out the observation. Pupils would naturally seek help from them and disturb the necessary concentration. The observation can be carried out by SENCO, head teacher or classroom assistant from another classroom or lesson.

The teacher of the focus lesson must have advance notice of observation. The observer should always be prepared to stop an observation if classroom circumstances are not conducive.

Ideally arrange a number of observations of the focus pupil in different lessons and at different times of the day. A single observation will provide useful but limited information.

Ensure that the target child does not know they are being observed. If the observer does not know how to recognise the child, the class teacher should be asked to speak to the focus child in a naturalistic way, using their name, two or three minutes after the observer has settled in the classroom.

The class teacher should be discouraged from talking about the focus child to the observer or physically pointing them out. However subtle and coded this sort of transaction is made, the children will be likely to pick up on it. After all, they are all keen to know why the observer is there and what they are about.

If the observer practises being unobtrusive and avoids interacting with teacher or children, the class will quickly ignore their presence and get on with the business of the lesson.

Procedure

The observer should sit some distance from the focus child but from where they can clearly see any work the child is doing.

Spend a few moments settling down and getting the feel of the classroom. This will allow the pupils to get used to their presence.

1. Be cordial but avoid communicating with pupils or teacher during this session.

2. Have a watch with a second hand which is clear to see.

3. Continually scan slowly around the classroom. As well as avoiding letting the focus child know they are being observed (that would clearly influence behaviour), a lot of additional information about the dynamics of the class group can be gleaned.

4. Record the last behaviour observed from the focus child and another child chosen at random (pupil A). Record one observation for each child alternately every 15 seconds. This gives an observation every 30 seconds per child.

5. Follow the key at the top of the record sheet. Record On Task, Off Task and Task-Related behaviour in the boxed columns provided.

6. Record individual teacher attention to each child using an asterisk at the side of the boxes provided. This will help later when interpreting the data because it is important to identify whether the child adjusted their attention to task in response to the teacher intervention.

7. Record any other brief information that you think will be important in the wider spaces on the chart, e.g. disrupting other pupils' work ... is being bullied by ... etc. Such observations need to be very brief. It may be helpful to develop some shorthand which can be easily interpreted later.

The observer can adapt the following list:

OOS	Out of seat
Disp	Dispute with child
ShO	Shouting
Dist	Disturbed other's work
Ch.	Chatting
Dyd	Daydreaming

8. At the end of the observation feed back to the class teacher a brief resume of the data.

9. Ask the class teacher to rate the pupil's performance in that lesson using the table at the bottom of the sheet.

10. Reward themselves with a cup of tea/coffee at the end of the observation because they will have worked very hard.

On-Task Behaviour Observation Record

Date ____/____/____   School _____   Lesson _____

Pupil's Task _____

Teacher _____   Observer _____

Time _____ to _____ Child A (Name _____) Child B (chosen at random).

✓	On Task
✗	Off Task
◯	Task Related
✱	Teacher Attention

General Observations

General Observations

5 Mins

10 Mins

15 Mins

20 Mins

Jonathan A Fogell

Teacher Evaluation: The pupil's behaviour this lesson presented:

[more problems than usual]   0   1   2   3   4   Average   6   7   8   9   10   [less problems tha

Appendix 2 – Personal Improvement Behaviour Programme

This behaviour programme is designed to enable the pupil and their teacher to monitor progress against agreed objectives over a period of time and to work towards an agreed reward. It can also help as a useful discussion point with parents.

Step One

1. Class teacher or form tutor to meet the pupil and to discuss with them any areas of concern in relation to pupil's classroom or playground behaviour. Where there are a wide number of concerns it will help to address the three main priority areas of concern. Where possible the pupil should be encouraged to identify the areas of concern and guidance should be given by the teacher. The teacher should aim to seek agreement with the pupil on the areas of concern by the end of the first discussion.

2. During this discussion any areas of concern to the pupil should be explored and possible strategies for alleviating the pupil's concerns discussed.

Step Two

Identifying objectives

Objectives can be identified in discussion with the pupil, focusing on clearly observable behaviours. They should be within the pupil's capabilities and, where possible, agreed rather than imposed by the teacher.

A sample set of objectives could be: Tristram to seek improvements in the following:

1. I listen attentively to the teacher when she is talking to me.

2. I get down to my work quickly.

3. I am friendly towards the other pupils in the class.

Agreed rewards

Teacher should discuss a range of rewards with the pupil. Ideally the reward on offer should be one that is important to the pupil but which is within the normal range of incentives for the classroom. Sample rewards could be:

1. 10 minutes extra time working on the computers.

2. One indoor break to play games etc.

3. A certificate or commendable behaviour slip.

4. A phone call home to parents.

5. To be allowed to carry out a valued task, e.g. operating the OHP at morning assemblies.

Monitoring

- Each teacher should rate pupil's progress against the above objectives at the end of each lesson. In small schools where the pupil sees relatively few teachers in their school day this is not difficult to arrange. In large schools all teachers working with the 'target pupil' should be informed of and encouraged to complete the record form at the end of each lesson. It may also help to give the pupil a short covering note to take around with them where they are likely to meet up with supply teachers.

- The scores are detailed on the monitoring sheet. They are nonetheless a subjective judgement by the teacher about the pupil's efforts in their lesson.

- It is important the monitoring sheets are used as discreetly as possible. It would not be a good idea, for example, to pin the sheets on display in the classroom unless the pupil particularly regards this as an incentive.

- At the end of each week points are totalled and if the pupil has got sufficient points the reward is given, if not then the process starts again the following week and the pupil is reminded of the importance of working towards the objectives.

Note

Behaviour Programmes are designed to bring about changes in pupil's behaviour. It is important that the time they are *formulated* (i.e. discussion between teacher and pupil) is noted as the start of the programme. The programme is then *implemented*. The record sheets are the process by which this behaviour programme is *monitored* and it should be *evaluated* at the end of each half term to ensure that it is bringing about improvements. If the pupil maintains a full term with improvements note, it is important to make a decision when to leave the behaviour programme. That change should be discussed with the pupil so that the stopping of the behaviour monitoring sheets is seen as a positive move.

Personal Improvement Chart

I am working hard to show improvements in the following:

1 _____

2 _____

3 _____

Ψ

Jonathan A Fogell 1996

Pupil's Name _____

Yr Group _____

Teacher's Name _____

Week starting _____

My teacher will give me points
for each lesson as follows:

excellent   = 3 points
very good = 2 points
good   = 1 point
ungraded   = 0 points

I have agreed with my teacher that if I
gain _____ points

I will receive the following:

	Monday	Tuesday	Wednesday	Thursday	Friday
1st am					
2nd am					
1st pm					
2nd pm					

Appendix 3 – Managing Stress

Coping With Stress

Pupils experiencing emotional and behavioural difficulties will often cause stress to both their peers and class teacher. On top of all the other pressures that are faced, an attention seeking or confrontational pupil can cause considerable concern. A teacher may have doubts about their ability to deal effectively with such problem behaviours and worry about the amount of time they are having to give to this one pupil. These concerns can so easily turn from being pressures into stressors with serious negative effects. Low self-esteem, self-defeating thoughts, physical symptoms of headaches and a reduced resistance to illness can all be indications of stress. (See below for symptoms and signs of stress.)

Every teacher is prone to stress. You may become negative, cynical and even hostile towards pupils and colleagues. THESE ARE STRESS REACTIONS. No one is immune.

The Best Person to Help Yourself Is You

The overall effect is clearly all round bad news for the teacher and all others involved, pupils, colleagues, as well as family and friends. We can imagine each of us carrying around a 'stress bucket' which each day gradually fills up as we meet the daily demands, until it over-spills in some way. We may displace our frustrations onto our family at home, or we overreact to some minor matter. A pupil with behavioural difficulties will fill the stress bucket all the more quickly.

Another helpful way of looking at stress is to imagine you are like the juggler at a circus trying to keep plates spinning in the air. You can manage any one of the plates, but as the numbers you are expected to keep up increases the pressure begins to tell. We manage through:

- letting some plates fall;

- only spinning the important ones;

- delegating some to others.

You may notice the effect of excessive pressure more through its absence. Do you find that three to four weeks into the summer holidays you begin to feel really relaxed and at ease with the world? This is because you are no longer using any energy to spin all those plates and the effort this was taking from you is free for other activities. Your muscles and mind are no longer constantly under pressure.

We need to take definite measures to ensure that we can manage our stress, rather than letting it spill over into problem symptoms.

A Six-Point Plan

Step 1 Accept and understand stress

At any time you will be faced with numerous demands and you will have to choose which to do and which to ignore. To deal with these pressures your body switches to 'red alert' and makes more energy available to you. Our nervous system was designed for the jungle where 'fight or flight' were the main options. These are obviously less appropriate today. As pressures increase our body tries to help through making more energy available for action. If we do not use it then that energy becomes tension in our muscles. Exercise of some kind is a key component of stress management.

Step 2 Recognise stress reactions

All of the caring professions are prone to these symptoms. For too long we have ignored the full effect teaching has on us. This is dramatically seen when we meet colleagues who retire or leave the profession. We meet them after some 12 months and do not recognise them. They look so well!

Physical/Doing do you experience:

- difficulties sleeping?

- muscle aches?

- dry mouth?

- sweating?

- frequent headaches?

- illnesses?

- unexplained tiredness?

- irritability?

- nervous habits?

- eating more/less?

- drinking more?

Thinking do you experience:

- concentration difficulties?

- making more mistakes and errors?

- finding it hard to make decisions?

- responding slowly to new situations?

- you can be erratic and impulsive?

- paranoid thoughts?

- self-defeating thoughts?

- irrational thoughts?

Emotions do you experience:

- low self-esteem?

- inability to switch off and relax?

- insensitivity to other people's needs?

- emotional outbursts?

- loss of interest in past pleasure pursuits?

- emotional lows?

Do you know your personal qualities and skills?
Can you recall a personal goal you recently achieved?
In which area of your life do you feel most competent?
How do you show your care for yourself and others?
Can you name a recent problem you managed well?

Personal support
Do you feel isolated and alone?
Do you have few people to turn to for emotional support?
Do you feel that most of your week is tied up with work?
Do you have few hobbies and relaxation activities?
Do you feel you are trapped in a rut?

Professional support
Do you have a colleague you can share concerns with?
Is there someone in school who will give you constructive feedback?
Do you have someone who respects your competence?
Do you have someone who will give you good information and assistance?
Are you aware of the kind of support you need?

Learn to relax. Learn new skills techniques and take a long-term perspective.

Step 6 Take action
Your action plan should be based on positive attitudes and good health. Within your school and local community there will exist support for you to make positive changes in your life. If you have read this seriously and know that it makes sense then, as no one else can do it for you, decide the first small step you need to do to begin and ...

DO IT NOW!

While your response is on account of external pressures you can be affected negatively. You should find out how your school or authority supports teachers under stress. Remember you are not on your own.

Teaching is a stressful profession and the increased pressures are causing stress to become too common an 'illness' for teachers.

STRESS IS A NORMAL REACTION
TO
ABNORMAL CIRCUMSTANCES

Essential Survival Tip
• Keep a sense of humour.

Appendix 4 – Lesson Behaviour Feedback Sheets

These sheets can be held by the teacher during lessons and marks discussed with the pupil at the end of each half day session. They can also be cut into separate lesson tickets and given to the pupil to hold to give them a clear visual cue to behaviour. These sheets are to be used to encourage positive behaviour and work effort from the pupil. They can also be used as a basis for negotiating reasonable targets with the pupil.

The way that feedback sheets are used should be decided by the class teacher and support staff in consultation with parents, SENCO, head teacher, psychologist or behaviour support service. The following is a suggested framework for their use.

1. Set clear achievable target behaviours for the pupil to work towards. If possible the targets should be achieved through a joint problem solving discussion.

2. Set clear rules which must be observed. If possible display the rules in the classroom.

3. Decide upon appropriate rewards and sanctions and the criteria for receiving them.

4. Agree a contingency plan with colleagues should the pupil continually get marks in the sanction zone. The contingency plan should be used immediately for severe behaviour, e.g. hitting other pupils.

5. Where possible ignore negative behaviour and celebrate positive behaviour.

6. Keep clear records of targets and progress.

Daily Use of the Sheets

These sheets are aimed at helping to overcome situations where pupils continually try to negotiate boundaries in the classroom. The reasons for and purpose of these sheets, and the overall behaviour support programme needs to be explained very clearly to the pupil. They are not aiming to provide a detailed evaluation of the pupil's performance. That can be done through the normal classroom processes. *They are aimed at providing clear visual indications of the teacher's level of satisfaction with the pupils' performance.* In particular they aim to provide positive reinforcement for good behaviour and good efforts. They also help to give early warning when the teacher is becoming concerned about the pupils' behaviour without the necessity to enter into a dialogue which can become negative.

- Every five to ten minutes the teacher puts an asterisk marker on the pupil's sheet to scale their level of contentment.

- Intervals between placement of markers should be varied and ad hoc. (This avoids the pupil trying to influence the position in which the teacher places the marker by short bursts of well-timed co-operation.)

- The positioning of any marker is non-negotiable and should involve minimal contact between the teacher and pupil.

- Discussion about progress can take place at the end of the lesson or other *agreed* time.

- If the sanction of removing the pupil from the lesson is used it must be non-negotiable, and, as a minimum, should last for the duration of the lesson in which it takes place.

- Return to the classroom should be negotiated between the pupil and the teacher and should be agreed by the teacher.

Every effort must be taken to avoid this process resulting in the pupil becoming 'singled out' or at risk of name calling from the other pupils. It is a positive tool. If it becomes negative it should be discontinued.

Jonathan A Fogell
Educational Psychologist
© January 1996

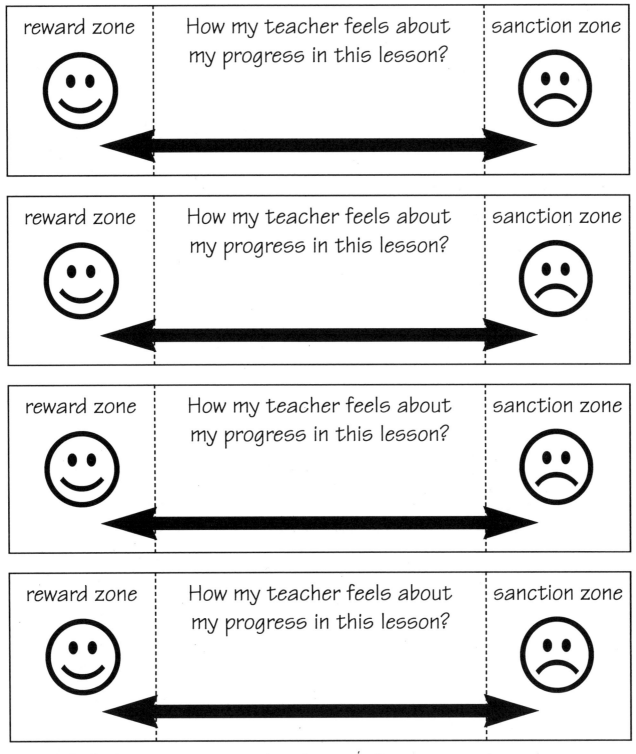

| reward zone | How my teacher feels about my progress in this lesson? | sanction zone |

Helping to get the best from my lessons

I am working to show improvements in: 1) _____

2) _____ 3) _____

stars in the reward zone will result in: _____

stars in the sanction zone will result in: _____

Appendix 5 – Rules Praise Ignore

This is a behavioural strategy which is based on the principles that i) children will behave better if the classroom rules are made explicit, ii) appropriate behaviour will be reinforced if it is praised and ii) poor behaviour will be diminished if it is not rewarded by teacher attention.

First stage of the procedure: RULES

Establishing the rules for each type of lesson may seem a laborious task. However, when this is done there can be no doubt as to what is expected of the children in the classroom. For the vast majority of children who are co-operating generally, this will come as no surprise and will present no difficulty. For those children who have problems in settling it will take away any doubt that may exist that the classroom rules are negotiable. (It is wise not to expect a dramatic change in behaviour as a result of this strategy. The effects tend to be cumulative. The process of making the rules explicit will serve as a constant reminder to all children of the acceptable boundaries of behaviour.)

In making the rules try to observe the following:

- Rules should be formulated with the class and posted where all can see them.

- Initially go over the rules three or four times, asking the class to repeat them back to you.

- Make the rules as short and to the point so they can be memorised easily by the children.

- Five or six rules (even less for infants) are enough.

- Where possible rules should be stated in positive terms: 'we work quietly' rather than 'we do not make a noise when we are working'.

- Keep a log of all the times that you review the classroom rules.

- Remind the class of the rules at times other than when someone has misbehaved.

Second stage: PRAISE

Make regular observations of the fact that children are keeping to the rules. Always complement the first child to be on-task and working appropriately. Make a point of announcing to the class when all of the pupils are on-task together. Give feedback at the end of a lesson on all of the pupils that have made a special effort to keep within the rules. (As always try to rein in those pupils who find it difficult to settle by strategic praise at a moment when they are co-operating.)

Third stage: IGNORE

If it is possible to ignore a minor transgression of the rules, do so. Clearly it is not possible to ignore behaviour which is abusive to other people or damaging to the property of others. It is better to deal quietly with transgressions separately from the class group and allow the overall social control to be based on praise and approval. It is also possible to deal with less serious transgressions with a referral to the rules or direction to the task rather than a rebuke for the transgression.

Rules Praise Ignore will not overcome a persistent and determined attempt by a pupil to disrupt a class. Other methods need to be used for such behaviour. It can, however, usefully reduce the incidence of minor disruptive behaviour and generate a more positive atmosphere in the classroom for all pupils by the controlling effect it has on those who find it harder to settle.

Appendix 6 – Pupil Planner

Guidelines

- Look for what is causing the pupil some distress or worry. These are usually good motivators.

- Actively involve the pupil in deciding the planner. They will follow their own plans far better.

- Help children teach you about who they are, practice listening skills. Listen so that they will talk – use active listening skills and encourage them to talk.

- Try to utilise the pupils' strengths in the programme.

- Make sure you agree targets, clearly and precisely.

- Record regularly the effect of what you are trying.

- Worry more about what the pupil is doing rather than what they are saying.

- Always make it explicit that they are OK, it is the behaviour you are concerned about.

- Ensure that you catch them succeeding, not failing.

- Make sure you know any key home circumstances etc.

- Make sure you are discussing your strategies with a colleague, friend or senior member of staff.

- Develop a positive attitude. Look each day for improvements.

- Remember that the Programme Planner is meant to record successes.

REMEMBER
CHILDREN ARE INVARIABLY
TRYING TO SOLVE PROBLEMS,
NOT BE A PROBLEM.

PUPIL PLANNER

NAME

What I would like to be better at:

A specific target I would like to work on:

What will help me get to my target?

What will hinder me?

Ideas that would help.

The Plan

I will ....

....

....

....

....

I will look at how matters are

going with ....

I agree to do this

....

If I have reached my target

I will...

Signed ....

Date...